Buying or Selling
a Home in
Northern Virginia

Buying or Selling a Home in Northern Virginia

by Betty Plashal

With

John Plashal

Gabriel Publications

Published by:
Gabriel Publications
14340 Addison St. #101
Sherman Oaks, California 91423
(818) 906-2147 Voice
(818) 990-8631 Fax
www.GabrielBooks.com

Copyright © 2006 Gabriel Publications
ISBN #1-891689-60-6
Library of Congress Catalog Card Number: 2005931284

Distributed by: Partners Book Distributors
Publisher: Rennie Gabriel
Editors: Davida Sims, David Robman and Nina Hickey
Typography: SDS Design, info@sds-design.com
Cover Design: Andres Plashal, Zeitgeist Media

Manufactured in the United States of America.

Dedication

I dedicate this book to the thousands of clients I have represented over the years. While buying or selling a home can be a stressful time for those involved, I have enjoyed my work thoroughly and it has been an honor to enter into and to become part of so many lives. I am truly grateful to have had an opportunity to assist so many individuals and families in the realization of their real estate dreams and goals.

Contents

Preface 9

Acknowledgments 11

Disclaimer 13

Map of Northern Virginia 15

About the Author. 17

  1. Northern Virginia. 19

  2. Benefits of Owning a Home:
Basics for First-Time Buyers and a
Refresher Course for Current Homeowners . . . 27

  3. Saving for the Purchase of a Home. 35

  4. "Visualizing" Your Future Home 43

  5. Real Estate and the Internet 51

  6. Finding a Good Realtor® 59

  7. How Much Home Can You Afford and
What's the Right Mortgage for You? 70

  8. How to Find a Good Lender 78

  9. Buying Your Home 94

10. Getting From the Contract to Closing 104

11. Selling Your Home. 128

12. Protecting Your Investment and
Upgrading Your Home 147

13. Investing in Real Estate in
Addition to Your Primary Residence 156

Appendix A: Glossary of Terms 169

Appendix B: Compendium of Useful Internet
Sites by Category 181

Appendix C: Handy "To Do" List
    for Your Move 185
Appendix D: Phone Lists 189
Appendix E: Preferred Partners 193

Preface

Welcome to an inside look at real estate in Northern Virginia—one of the most dynamic areas in America and home to well over two million residents. This book will give you all the information you need to be an informed homebuyer or home seller in Northern Virginia. It can be used as a guide by the first time homebuyer, as an introduction course to the real estate market, or as a valuable resource for "veteran" homeowners who are considering another move. No matter which of these categories you fall into, this book will give you valuable information. You can read it from cover to cover or refer to the chapters that especially apply to your situation. However you approach this learning experience, I promise that you will walk away with all of the basic information that you need to be prepared for any real estate transaction in Northern Virginia.

If your primary goal at this time is to sell your home, for example, you probably also are planning on buying another. Thus literally every chapter in this book will be of interest to you, not just the one focused on selling your house. By reading this book you will be equipped to make a smart decision on whether buying or selling real estate in Northern Virginia is the right choice for you, and you can develop a plan outlining the most time-effective and profitable way to go about it.

In what follows, I present the reader with advice on the financial, practical and emotional side of the home buying experience. This book also includes:

- A glossary detailing all of the technical terms involved in the real estate process.

- Information on the wide range of technical issues involved in real estate transactions and advice on how to find a good lender and Realtor®.

- Appendixes that list helpful websites for researching potential neighborhoods; provide phone numbers and email addresses for key services including electricity, gas, water utilities, and school boards; and provide a checklist for the many details you must handle when moving.

- Advice on having a lifetime "real estate plan".

In summary, this book presents an overview of "big picture" issues regarding your financial and real estate objectives, explains the practical issues involved in navigating those waters, and provides a valuable database that can be consulted time and again over the years.

Acknowledgments

Acknowledgments by Betty Plashal

I would like to thank a number of individuals who provided important insight and improvements to the original manuscript.

Specifically, I would like to thank **Pat Paulas** of Long and Foster Realtors, a fellow Realtor® and member of Teamworks, **Dave McWatters** of Long and Foster Realtors, **Carl Gamlen** of Prosperity Mortgage, **Patrick Wyman** of RGS Title, **Ryan Jackson** of TCB Consulting, Inc., **Ms. Linda Braley** of Linda Braley Real Estate Appraisal Services, Inc., **Dorothy Mathers**, a former client, **Tim Starinieri** of PropPrep Tax and Accounting Services, Inc., who reviewed the tax information in the book, **Drew Paulas** of Foliographics, Inc., of Sterling, Virginia, who designed the map, and **Andres Plashal** of Zeitgeist Media, for his fine work on designing the book's cover.

I also extend special thanks and appreciation to **Laura Reed-Morrisson**, who did such a great job in editing the final manuscript.

It is a humbling experience to have one's final draft improved through rearranged paragraphs, alternative words and phrases, corrected spellings, and a host of other changes.

Disclaimer

Although the information in this book is as accurate and as current as possible, laws are constantly changing and circumstances will always vary, so there is no way to ensure up to the minute complete accuracy on legal and technical factors and there is always the possibility for error. I advise you to use the information in this book as a guide, but make sure that you always consult a professional for questions regarding your specific situation. If your situation is complicated by factors such as your property having a septic tank, a well or unique title issues, I recommend you consult with an expert who specializes in those issues. You may want to hire an attorney or other professional who can assist with the specifics involved. This book is NOT providing legal advice. The views expressed in these pages are my personal observations based on many years of work in the residential real estate market and do not necessarily reflect the views of Long and Foster Realtors or its affiliates.

About gender usage: In order to avoid numerous grammatical messes and to make the reading flow better, I have chosen to write this book as gender neutral as possible. I use *they* and *their*, even if it is one person, instead of *he or she, his and hers* and so on.

About the term *Realtor*®: This is a registered trademark of the National Association of REALTORS® (NAR), and anyone who uses that term as part of their professional identity must be a member, not only of the NAR but also of their local and state associations. I always encourage both buyers and sellers to seek out the services of a

Realtor® when possible. You can also feel free to contact me directly if you have questions, or if you need a referral to a Realtor® anywhere in the United States. To make the text easier to read I will show the registration mark following the lowercased term *Realtor®*, and I also use the term *agent*.

Map of Northern Virginia

As the map below shows, Northern Virginia borders on Washington D.C., and the state of Maryland. In addition to the cities of Alexandria, Fairfax and Manassas, the counties considered to be part of Northern Virginia include Arlington, Fairfax, Loudoun, Prince William, Stafford and Spotsylvania. A few years ago the last two counties mentioned above would not have been considered the suburbs of Washington D.C. However, the population explosion in those counties and their dramatic commercial expansion has integrated them into the regional economy as these two formerly rural counties continue to rapidly urbanize.

The lower cost of land in the outlying counties has drawn many new homebuilders and their customers. The upsurge in employment opportunities throughout the Northern Virginia area (see Chapter 1) has also added to the appeal of living in counties which are somewhat distant from the city of Washington.

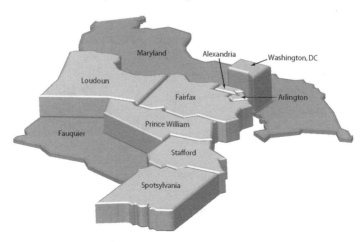

About the Author

BETTY PLASHAL started her real estate career with Long and Foster Realtors in the 1970s, shortly after the company was formed. The company was founded by Wes Foster and Henry Long and originally was just a two-man office. Today, under Wes Foster's ownership, the corporation operates in a number of Mid-Atlantic states and had sales of over $40 billion in 2004. It is the largest independently owned real estate company in America.

In her first year with the company, Betty was named "Rookie Agent of the Year." She has been the company's Top Producing Agent on a number of occasions, and during her career she has sold or listed more than 3,000 properties. Betty has received more than one hundred awards and letters of recognition, including being named the "Salesperson of the Year" for the Northern Virginia Association of Realtors®. She has continued her education in real estate over the years and has achieved many designations, including Associate Broker, Certified Residential Specialist (CRS), the Graduate Realtor® Institute (GRI), and is an Internet Certified Professional (e-PRO). She consistently ranks as a leader in the Dulles Area Association of Realtors® and has served as a director for the association for five years.

One of Betty's proudest achievements was receiving the coveted Herman Methfessel Service award. This award is presented each year to one Long and Foster employee. Herman was the vice president of Long and Foster for many years. The award recognizes Betty for her

"Outstanding Service to Her Clients, Fellow Agents and Community".

Her commitment to the education of new real estate agents has been a priority throughout Betty's career. A former schoolteacher, she never lost the desire to teach—she has taught new agent courses and has personally mentored new agents over the years. Betty also founded a marketing network group of Realtors®, lenders and builders called SHARE. This group formed as a networking group with monthly educational meetings during the late 1980s, a time of recession in real estate.

Betty's real estate practice specializes in both marketing residential homes and representing buyers in the purchase of homes in Northern Virginia. She worked with a real estate partner, Patricia Johnston, for many years. When Pat moved to Arizona, Betty teamed up with Patricia Paulas and an administrative assistant, Joyce Schuler. This group is called *Teamworks*. Our website (which is continually updated) is *www.callteamworks.com*.

To Reach Betty Plashal:
Email: theTeam@CallTeamworks.com
Office: (703) 444-TEAM (8326)
Cell: (703) 926-8177

1

Northern Virginia

Northern Virginia is one of the finest places to live in America. Its location and fantastically dynamic economy are among its major advantages. Being just across the Potomac River from one of the world's greatest cities—Washington, D.C.—helps place it in one of the strongest regional economies in the country. The strength of the Northern Virginia economy is demonstrated by its unemployment rate, which was recently below 2 percent. Homes in the region have increased dramatically in value and always rank near the top, nationwide, in the percentage increased value of residential properties.

The quality of life in Northern Virginia—no matter which measurement you use—is exceptional. The climate is moderate, and many winters produce only a few serious snows. The per capita income is one of the highest in the nation. The education levels of the populace and the quality of the schools rank at or near the top when compared to any other area of the country. The fine beaches of the Atlantic Ocean are a short drive away. Similarly, ski resorts in Virginia, West Virginia and Pennsylvania are also just a few hours away.

The region's cultural life is rich, diverse and lively. In recent years, over $1 billion has been spent on new museums—including the National Museum of the American Indian on the Mall, the Steven F. Udvar-Hazy Center at the National Air and Space Museum located near the Dulles airport, and the Spy Museum in Washington, D.C. A number of other museums are in various stages of going forward; some are almost fully funded, and others are in the planning stage. These include the National Museum of the U.S. Army, a National Music Center and Museum, The Cold War Museum, a National Health Museum, the National Women's History Museum, and a Marine Corps Museum. These new and future museums are, of course, merely adding to the enormous wealth of existing ones, including the Smithsonian Air and Space Museum, the National Museum of Natural History, the United States Holocaust Memorial Museum, the Hirshhorn Museum and Sculpture Garden, the National Museum of African Art and the National Portrait Gallery.

Moreover, world-class performances take place year-round at the John F. Kennedy Center for the Performing Arts, the National Theater, the Arena Theater, the Wolftrap Theater (with its delightful outdoor performances), and the Shakespeare Theater in downtown D.C. There are also scores of neighborhood theaters. For those who are longtime residents of the metropolitan area and frequently visit these magnificent resources, congratulations! To those of you who have resided here for years but do not participate in this plethora of cultural opportunities, I encourage you to think of the slogan of a certain national company and "just do it."

However, the area's cultural riches are not simply measured by museums and venues for the performing arts. Embassies from almost every country in the world are located in Washington (over 170, and an equal number of ambassadors' residences). They are located in neighborhoods that are just a subway ride or a short car trip away from Northern Virginia.

If dining out is an important part of your lifestyle, you are in the right place. The restaurant sections in the Yellow Pages for Northern Virginia, suburban Maryland, and Washington, D.C., total just over 100 pages of addresses and ads. Any cuisine you can imagine or desire is located in the area.

Major universities in the region include George Mason, Georgetown, the University of Maryland, American University, Howard University, the Catholic University of America, and Marymount University. Widely varied two-year community colleges, computer schools and business schools, all of high quality, are conveniently located throughout the area. The scope of the medical facilities and resources in the region is remarkable, with specialists on every conceivable illness, dozens of hospitals, and world-renowned research facilities such as the National Institutes of Health in suburban Maryland and the Johns Hopkins medical complex in nearby Baltimore, just 30 miles away.

Professional sports teams include the Washington Redskins football team, the Washington Capitals hockey team, the Washington Nationals baseball team, the Washington Wizards men's basketball team, and the Washington Mystics women's basketball team. There are approximately 100 golf courses in the region and many thousands of acres of parks.

To sum up—Northern Virginia is a great place to live!

Changing Economic Landscape

Northern Virginia has seen an enormous increase in the number and size of corporations specializing in a variety of high-tech fields, including telecommunications, homeland security, and information technology.

Chapter 1

Recently, Governor Mark Warner announced that 11,000 new homeland security jobs would be created in Northern Virginia as four large companies with contracts expand their workforces. The average annual salary of these jobs is projected to be $79,000. In addition, the scheduled opening of a major biomedical research facility in Loudoun County, funded by the Howard Hughes Foundation, will represent an important new growth industry in the area. Recent data revealed that the number of jobs in the entire metropolitan Washington area grew by more than 80,000 in the past year. Due to the explosive growth of the private sector during the past 15 years or so (as opposed to the earlier traditional expansion of government jobs in the region), the square footage of commercial property in Northern Virginia is now 32 percent greater than all of the office space in the city of Washington, D.C. This affects lifestyle and home values for Northern Virginia residents in a positive way.

As recently as the 1970s, the value of homes in the Virginia suburbs was greatly impacted by how far the residence was located from the employment center of Washington, D.C. Now, however, there are numerous massive "nodes"—that is, concentrated areas—of employment throughout the region. You can best visualize the economic dynamics of Northern Virginia by noting that there are four major economic/employment nodes: the Pentagon–Crystal City corridor, the Rossyln-Ballston Corridor, the Tysons Corner to Dulles Airport corridor, and the "West End" of Alexandria. If you live in Northern Virginia, the odds are quite high that you will be employed in one of these locations or in Washington, D.C.

These employment nodes are not simply a sprinkling of office parks. They are massive complexes that employ tens of thousands of people. The Pentagon, which employs 25,000 people, is just blocks away from the massive Crystal City office complex. Tyson Corners is an office/shopping center complex located next to the

Beltway. Two shopping centers at this location, *Tyson Corners Center* and *The Galleria*, are among the largest in the nation, and Tyson's also has 20 million square feet of office space.

Given the locations of these employment nodes, Northern Virginia residents have a wide choice of neighborhoods and often can live relatively near their places of employment. Much of the growth has occurred in recent years. Virginia's Loudoun County, for example, was the fastest-growing county in America between 2000 and 2003. In 2003 Spotsylvania County became the nineteenth-fastest-growing county in the country. Prince William County is undergoing a dramatic economic expansion. These statistics also mean, of course, that a large percentage of the region's housing stock is quite new.

Also, a major new employment node will emerge in the next number of years. The Department of Defense recently recommended to the Base Realignment and Closure Commission that many of the office buildings in Northern Virginia—currently occupied with various agencies or corporations carrying out military related functions—should have their operations moved to a vast new complex which would be constructed at Fort Belvoir in Northern Virginia. Reportedly, as this plan goes forward, up to 20,000 jobs would be relocated to Fort Belvoir. Congress is expected to approve this plan.

OK! OK! It's Not Heaven on Earth

Having listed so many of the advantages of living in Northern Virginia, it is only fair to point out two drawbacks: the cost of real estate and the traffic.

Home Prices

If you're moving to Northern Virginia from Los Angeles, the New York City region, or San Francisco, you will not be shocked at the prices. Indeed, in some cases, you may be able to buy more home for the dollar than you can where you currently reside. On the other hand, if you're moving to Northern Virginia from say Star Prairie, Iowa, get ready for sticker shock.

A number of years ago, I had an out-of-state client who was moving to the area from Kansas. He and his wife met me at my office and told me that they were willing to pay up to $250,000 for a home, but wanted a lot of three to five acres and a colonial-style residence. Sadly, I had to inform them that I was aware of some attractive multi-acre lots in nice neighborhoods that were selling for around $250,000—but those lots did not yet have any homes on them! The little detail of building a home on the lot would involve substantial additional costs.

Commuting

There is no getting around it: rush hour can be very time-consuming, depending on your situation. You can minimize the inconvenience of a long commute, however. One obvious way is to live near your employer. As I noted above, numerous employment nodes are located throughout Northern Virginia. Many federal agencies are actually located in the Virginia suburbs, not in Washington, D.C. The Pentagon, which is the largest building in the world in terms of square footage (it has one-third more square footage than the 110 floor Sears Tower), is located on the Virginia side of the Potomac River; the Central Intelligence Agency is in McLean, Virginia; the United States Patent and Trademark Office is in Alexandria, Virginia; the National Reconnaissance Office (classified satellite programs) is in Centreville, Virginia; the National Science Foundation is in Arlington, Virginia; and the Interior Department's U.S. Geological Survey office is in Reston, Virginia.

America Online's headquarters is more than twenty miles from Washington, D.C. The Dulles International Airport, also over 20 miles from Washington, is the fifth-busiest airport in America, and has thousands of employees. The corridor from Tyson Corners to the Dulles airport has innumerable office buildings. In many cases, then, you can live a great distance from the city of Washington and still have a short commute to work.

If living relatively close to your place of employment is, for whatever reason, not a viable option, a second way to minimize your commute is to use the Metro—the Washington-area subway. It is the second-largest subway system in the nation, with a daily ridership of more than 600,000. There are 84 Metro stations, and currently, 20 of these are located in Virginia. The distance of your residence from a Metro stop can have a significant impact both on your lifestyle and on the value of your property. There are huge developments—condominiums, office buildings, and apartment complexes—in the neighborhoods surrounding many of the Metro stations in Virginia.

A number of years ago two of my clients, Bill and Kathleen Ricketts, purchased a home that was located about six blocks from the Nutley Station metro stop in Vienna. The home they bought was (at that time) a modestly priced split-level, built in the 1950s on a half-acre treed lot. I went to their home for lunch recently and barely recognized the neighborhood. Builders were buying the older homes, knocking them down, and putting up *two* $900,000 "McMansions" or "Starter Castles" (as some irreverently refer to them) on *each* of the half-acre lots. The new homes were selling quickly, as they had all the new-home amenities *plus* the advantage of being within walking distance of a subway station.

The initial phase of the planned extension of the Metro to the Dulles airport—which is currently 12 miles from the nearest Metro stop—has been funded. Eleven new stations are planned for this proposed extension, and their locations have already been designated. As this project goes forward, I feel certain that those who have the fortune and the foresight to own homes reasonably close to these future subway stations will see a dramatic appreciation in the value of their properties.

In addition to the METRO, another mass transit option is the Virginia Railway Express (VRE). The VRE commuter trains travel on Norfolk Southern tracks. There are a total of 18 VRE stations, including 16 in Northern Virginia and two in Washington, which are located at transportation nodes and office complexes.

2

Benefits of Owning a Home: Basics for First-Time Buyers and a Refresher Course for Current Homeowners

When you make the decision to purchase your first home (or move from your current home to another one), you will begin a true adventure. Not only will your choice have a major impact on your lifestyle, but it will also be one of the three most important financial decisions you will make in your lifetime. The others, of course, are choosing your career and having a sound retirement plan. Here are some of the advantages to homeownership.

Leverage

First, you should be aware of the importance of leverage. For a very small down payment—or, in some cases, no down payment—you can acquire a very expensive asset. It doesn't take a Ph.D. in math to calculate the importance of leverage to your prospects for long-term wealth.

Obviously, there can be no guarantee of future appreciation. However, for discussion purposes, let's say you are purchasing a $300,000 residence, and your down payment is $15,000. Let's also say that your home appreciates at 5 percent per year during the first three years. (Using this number is very conservative. Appreciation in Northern Virginia actually has been considerably higher than that in recent years. In fact, it has surpassed 20 percent in 2004 in some areas.) Let's look at the numbers with just 5 percent annual appreciation.

	Value of Home (5% Increase)	Increase in Equity
End of first year	$315,000	$15,000
End of second year	330,750	30,750
End of third year	347,290	47,290

Eureka! In this case, by the end of the third year of your homeownership, your total equity is $62,290—consisting of your $15,000 down payment and your $47,290 increase in equity. These figures do not include the incremental equity you will have built up from paying down the principal on your mortgage. The return of your investing $15,000 in a home and having over $62,000 in equity after three years sure beats investing that $15,000 in a bank's certificate of deposit yielding 3 percent a year (or about $450 per year over that time period). By the way, the above-described increase in your net worth does not factor in another advantage: tax breaks that further enhance your wealth through homeownership.

Tax Advantages

Capital Gains

The term *capital gain* refers in general to the difference between what you pay for an asset and the price at which you sell it. The IRS uses this difference in price to measure your profit (i.e., gains from an investment of capital) and thus your tax liability. If you own stocks, mutual funds, or bonds (outside of a retirement plan), the government taxes your long-term capital gain at a rate of 15 percent when you sell the investment.

In 1997, as part of the Taxpayer Relief Act, Congress created a provision that eliminates the federal income tax liability on the capital gain on the sale of a principal residence (with some caps and restrictions). Under the new law, if you meet certain qualifications, up to $250,000 of the gain from the sale of a single person's principal residence is tax-free. And for married couples filing a joint tax return, the amount of tax-free gain doubles to $500,000—a substantial amount of tax-free money!

Prior to this change, homeowners had to "roll over" or "buy up" in order to defer their gain to a later tax year. Also gone are the "over-age-55, once-in-a-lifetime" rules regarding a gain. *The new exclusion is for everyone and can be used repeatedly as long as the home is your principal residence and you own and reside in it for at least two of the last five years.*

The rules allowing you to take your home-sale profits tax-free apply regardless of your age and regardless of how many homes you might sell in the future or have sold in the past. It is available even if you previously qualified for and took a "once-in-a-lifetime" tax exclusion on a prior home sale. As long as you qualify and meet the residency requirements outlined in the tax law, this exclusion is available.

Additionally, even if you have lived in the primary residence for less than two years, you may be able to take advantage of a deduction for the percentage of time that you lived in the house, if your move is related to work or health issues. For more information on how these situations can lead to possible tax exclusions, it is best to contact your accountant.

Finally, remember that any gain in excess of the exclusion amount will be subject to a 15 percent taxation rate. You cannot "roll over" any additional gain into a new residence, because those prior rollover rules are no longer in force. Check out IRS Publication 17, Part Three, for more detail. Another pertinent IRS document is Publication 523 *Selling Your Home*. Even though a CPA has reviewed this information, make sure you consult your own tax adviser on real estate tax issues.

Mortgage Interest Deduction

Along with getting tax-free money when you sell your primary residence, you can deduct the interest you pay on your mortgage on your annual income tax return. You should not underestimate the value of this deduction, which can be particularly lucrative in your first years of homeownership because 90 to 95 percent of your monthly payments represent interest. On a 30-year fixed loan, banks charge the bulk of the interest up front. If you sell your home in the first few years after you buy it, the bank will still realize a good return on its investment.

Conversely, of course, while you will not build up much equity in the first few years because of a lower balance on the principal, you will build significant equity through your home's appreciation. Here is an example of how this works. Let's say that your monthly mortgage payment is $1,500, of which $1,420 is interest. At the end of the year, you can claim a $17,040 deduction on your tax return. Additionally, you can deduct property taxes. Not bad, considering that we are dealing with the IRS!

But stand by. There is one more advantage beyond all of these.

Psychological Advantage

There is an important psychological element to buying real estate. Owning your own little piece of the planet is great for the psyche! Let's face it—most folks like to own "stuff". While some may get carried away with accumulating too much, it is a basic human instinct to want to own your own property.

A few years ago, when my husband and I bought two investment properties (townhouses in Loudoun County), the lawyer at the settlement told us a touching story. She had recently been the settlement attorney for a home a U.S. immigrant had bought. He was married and had two children.

This new homebuyer brought a video camera and a friend to videotape the entire settlement process. Folks, trust me, there is nothing very exciting or even remotely interesting about the settlement procedures formalizing the purchase of a home. A lawyer or a settlement agent goes over page after page of legal papers that must be signed to "dot the *I's* and cross the *T's*" in the process of legalizing the transaction. The immigrant's friend videotaped the purchaser's entrance into the law firm, recording the whole settlement process as well as brief conversations with the back-office personnel. The new homeowner undoubtedly sent copies of the video back to his relatives and friends in his home country. He was not only buying a home *he was buying a home for his family in America*!

"Honey, I Have a Plan: Let's Buy One Share of Stock"

Here is a unique way to conceptualize your home purchase. You are buying one share of a company's stock. You love that stock—which in effect is your home, condo or townhouse—and you plan to buy "one whole share" eventually, giving you complete ownership.

Complete ownership of one share of the stock would currently cost $300,000, and all you have is $15,000. So a second party (the mortgage lender) agrees that $15,000 is all you need to buy a portion of that share. As part of the deal, however, you must agree to buy another small portion of that single share of stock each month until you either agree to sell the portion of the share you own or until you own that share completely.

During the time you partially own that share, you and your family are living in that share and getting a tax break for your partial ownership. That share is also steadily increasing in value. When you sell it, there are no taxes on your gains unless your share has increased by more than a half-million dollars for a couple. *Is this a great country, or what?*

Be Realistic

Rest assured, homeownership can be very rewarding if you take some time to evaluate your priorities, obligations and long-term objectives. However, you should always be realistic in setting your real estate goals—make sure that you understand and calculate the expenses that go with a home purchase.

- Your monthly expenses—not just your monthly mortgage payment—may increase when you buy a home. Utilities will probably cost more and, of course, there will be the upkeep of the home. When something breaks, you (not a landlord) will be responsible for fixing it.

- If you have a mortgage, you will be required to have homeowner's insurance and, of course, you also pay property taxes.

- Your transportation costs may increase if you move farther away from your work.

Next, look at your current financial situation and consider your lifestyle.

- Are you considering making a career change that warrants a return to school? Will the career change result in a temporary pay cut?

- Do you take a major vacation each year? Will you still be able to do so once you buy a home? (If you can't, how will you feel about it?)

- What expenses can you cut back on while maintaining a reasonable lifestyle?

- Do you have a backup fund to take care of emergencies?

- Do you need to save for your children's college education?

- How much money goes toward funding your retirement?

- What other personal financial obligations must you meet each month?

A lender can tell you the mortgage amount you can afford based on your financial report. Only you, however, know how homeownership and the expenses involved fit into your overall financial picture and goals.

You must determine whether making contributions to your retirement or saving for that special vacation must be put on hold if you borrow the mortgage amount for which you're approved. Do your homework, and start by looking at your total financial picture. Don't "fall in love" and purchase a home that seriously strains your finances simply because you can afford it on paper.

3

SAVING FOR THE PURCHASE OF A HOME

The easiest way to build assets for the purchase of a home is to own a home already appreciating in value. Anyone who has owned a home in the Northern Virginia region over the past few years has built up substantial equity, giving them a nice "savings pool" as a down payment for the purchase of the next home. If you are a potential homebuyer with considerable equity in your current residence, you can fast forward to the next chapter. If you are a first-time buyer with minimal assets and various debts, however, read on.

Often, first-time buyers face the challenge of accumulating assets and minimizing their liabilities as they strive to get into the home market. While your current financial situation is central to your plan for purchasing a home, you should not become overly concerned. You may be earning an excellent income, but feel it's not enough to save for a down payment. Or you may be struggling to get by and don't know where to start. Regardless of your circumstances, you can start the process of saving for a home. You don't need to save 20 percent or even 10 percent of the purchase price before you start thinking about buying a home. Today, first-time buyers are able to buy homes (at reasonable interest rates) with as little as 3 to 5 percent down. In some cases, *no* down payment is required. You may only need the closing costs of the loan to purchase your first home. But you will need *some* cash.

Where do you start if you have no assets and, indeed, you are in debt? It's simple. You create a practical, step-by-step approach based on your financial history and stay with your plan until you realize your goal. As with all things in life, perseverance will pay off.

The key to setting financial goals is to be specific. Effective goals need to be SMART: *Specific, Measurable, Action-oriented, Realistic and Time-limited.*

Specific

Set a specific goal. You can say, "I don't want to live in my apartment anymore." But what does that really mean? Do you want to buy a house? How much do you want to spend? Will a condo or townhouse fit your needs?

Measurable

Simply saying that you don't want to live in your apartment—or move to another apartment—is not good enough. If you say, "I will find a home in a price range I can afford within six months," then you will have something by which to measure your success. You have to start by creating the measurement.

Action-oriented

The goal is not static: it involves *doing* something. Do not use the words "going to," as in "I'm going to be rich." Without taking action, you are always "going" somewhere—but you never arrive.

Realistic

Talk to a Realtor® or a loan officer to determine what your near-term financial goals will have to be in order to qualify for a home loan.

Time-limited

A goal is nothing more than a dream with a deadline attached.

Getting Started

Once you have set your goal, you'll need to start outlining how you will achieve it. But before you do, two other important lessons will help you along the way.

First, in order to reach a goal, it's best to have other people involved. Share with other people. Do not work on it alone; have other people value your goal, too. The people you work with, or your spouse and friends, can help you focus on making your goal specific and measurable. They can question you about being realistic and having a deadline, and they will support you in getting what you want. You can also use the experience of others. You may save yourself some painful lumps if you learn what worked, or didn't work, for others. (Try to determine how similar your situation is to the frame of reference you're using.)

Second, track your results. Take the time to write down the small steps taken toward your goal in a calendar or appointment book. If you set a realistic goal and track your progress, you can modify or evaluate your progress continually until you eventually meet your goal!

Tips on Meeting Your Goals

Know where your money is going, and address this honestly and meticulously. You cannot realize any goal without first finding out your starting point. You may not know all the numbers, so "ballpark" them and go to the next step to find out how to get more concrete answers.

Types of Monthly Expenses

Learn to understand the categories of your various types of monthly expenses—*discretionary, variable* and *fixed. Discretionary* expenses are the ones over which you have complete control. They may include going to the movies, meals out, personal trainers, vacations, clothing or lottery tickets, for example. *Variable* expenses show up every month. The only difference is the amount of the expense. As an example, you'll have a food bill every month, but it could be higher or lower from one month to the next based on what you buy. Your utility bills, such as telephone, gas and electric, will come in month after month, but they may be higher or lower depending on your usage or the season. Finally, *fixed* expenses come in every month and do not change. Rent or mortgage payments, car payments and insurance premiums fall into this category. (It could also include the minimum payment on credit cards, but even these can be changed.) Note, too, that while rent is a fixed expense, you could consider getting a roommate for a period of time as a means of building up your savings and cutting your expenses.

Getting Out of Debt

If reorganizing or consolidating your debts or selling assets isn't enough to get your financial house in order, you may need to consult a financial planner or a credit-assistance organization such as the Consumer Credit Counseling Service.

Millions of Americans have too much credit card debt, which limits their buying power and their ability to save for a down payment. If you fall into this category, let me assure you that saving is possible. Let's start by looking at the different levels of credit card debt.

Level one credit card debt is debt that you pay off monthly. This would include any credit card account that carries no balance into the next month. *Level two* credit card debt occurs when you carry debt from month to month, but you regularly make payments above the minimum. At *level three* credit card debt, you are only able to make minimum payments on your credit cards. And at *level four*, you cannot make those minimum payments.

Now let's say that you are trying to save for a home and your credit card debt is mostly at level three (that is, you can just make your minimum payments). You still have options. You may want to consider a consolidation loan, look around for a low-interest credit card, or call your current creditors and ask them to reduce your interest rates. If they agree to do so, make sure that you do not reduce your payments just because they've lowered the interest rates. Maintain your payment level and you'll eliminate the debt sooner.

What if you're at level four and you can't even make the minimum payments? A book by Jerrold Mundis called *How to Get Out of Debt, Stay Out of Debt, and Live Prosperously* may be useful to you. Regardless of whether you're at level two, three or four, do not add any new debt while paying off your current or old debt.

If you pay off your debt the "quick and easy" way, that debt invariably returns. People who borrow against the equity in their home or refinance it, receive an inheritance or tax refund, win the lottery, get a gift from parents or others, declare bankruptcy or get a consolidation loan to deal with what they owe *have learned no new skills to pay off debt*. Such maneuvers do not produce the necessary skills. Rather, people learn to use similar tactics to get themselves out of debt the next time! Creating financial independence comes from learning to handle money effectively.

Pay Yourself First

Pay yourself first. Pay yourself before you pay the telephone bill or pay for groceries, rent or transportation expenses. If you want to feel that you are moving toward your goal, you have to see the results in the bank—that means paying yourself first. After you've paid yourself, then pay your expenses. These will include your credit card or other debts, but when they're paid off you can dramatically increase the amount you pay yourself.

The average person spends first and then finds that about 10 to 20 percent of his or her income disappears. If you pay yourself first, all you will lose out on spending is that 10 to 20 percent that would have been lost regardless. Even if all you can start with is setting aside 10 percent of your income, then you are at least on your way to that down payment. Remember, any allocation is better than none at all.

Once you start saving—and, more important, once you have a savings plan—you will know how much money you can afford to put down on a house. Maybe it is more than you think. And there are loan programs out there for almost anyone. Now is the time to make the commitment to saving so that you can soon make the commitment to buying a home!

Knowing Your Credit Score

Obviously, maintaining good credit is essential. You may be unaware of how many organizations access and use your credit information to make decisions that affect you. In addition to those you would expect to check on you—such as a credit card issuer, department store, mortgage lender or car dealer—your credit may also be checked by a new employer, life or auto insurance company, or prospective landlord. Issuers of homeowner's insurance also check credit ratings and may refuse to issue a new policy or renew your existing policy. You can understand, then, how others see your good credit as a reflection of who you are as a person.

One of the primary methods the mortgage lending industry uses to assess your credit worthiness is your FICO score. (FICO stands for Fair Isaac Corporation, which developed and keeps a classified scoring system.) A FICO score is a numeric score that summarizes your credit history and is maintained by credit reporting companies. FICO uses different models and adjusts the score depending on a variety of factors, such as your amount of credit, any bankruptcy you have had, how many credit cards you have with no balance or how many credit cards you have with high balances. FICO is a third party that provides these scores to a potential lender. The lender does not calculate the score but uses it to establish a borrower's creditworthiness. You can get more information from their website at *www.fairisaac.com.*

A score in the range of 660–700 is good and would allow the potential borrower to qualify for a loan ranked as A, which would have the lowest interest rates and most favorable terms. If a mortgage rate of 6.5 percent were the best available rate at that time, a person with an A score would qualify for that rate. If the score were around 620–650, that person would qualify for B- or a B+ loan, and the interest rate would be higher. With a score of 580–620, a borrower would fall in the C range and find that the interest rate offered would be significantly higher than the best rates. These loans are "subprime"; only certain mortgage companies specialize in them. Lower scores mean higher fees, too. Obviously, the opposite is also true—the higher your score, the better the terms of the mortgage and the easier it will be to qualify. (The "scoring system" actually goes to 850.)

Regardless of your situation, you should get a copy of your credit report every year to make sure that all of the information is correct. It is important to note that your FICO score is affected each time there is an inquiry from a lender checking on your credit worthiness. If you get a copy of your credit report, please use that exact report as you search for a lender. Do not allow every lender to search your credit worthiness by running a credit report because if this happens, your score gets lowered. I discuss this issue in Chapter 8, *How to Find a Good Lender.*

You are entitled to one free credit report a year from the three major credit bureaus—Equifax, Experian and Trans Union:

Equifax PO Box 105873 Atlanta, GA 30348
800-685-1111

Experian PO Box 2104 Allen, TX 75013
888-682-7654

Trans Union PO Box 390 Springfield, PA 19064
800-888-4213

In addition, because of a recent amendment to the federal Fair Credit Reporting Act (FCRA), you can get a free credit report annually through the Annual Credit Report Request Service. This is currently available only to folks living in the western United States, but by September 1, 2005, it will be available nationwide. Contact the service at Central Credit Report Data Bank, *www.annualcreditreport.com.*

Annual Credit Report Request Service
P.O. Box 105281, Atlanta Georgia 30348-5281
(877) 322-8228

4

"Visualizing" Your Future Home

Whether you are a first-time buyer or have bought a number of homes over the years and are about to make another move, as you begin the process of getting serious about your home purchase, you should start by "visualizing" the home you intend to buy. You should put on paper every single feature that you want in your next residence. Maybe you want an extra-large kitchen with an attached family room. Perhaps you prefer a large condo that is located in the heart of the city. Think hard, because although you may not be able to find or afford everything you desire, compiling such a list will help both you and your agent know what residence will best meet your needs.

Once you have your list, the next step is to narrow your focus down to the items you can and can't live without. If you are buying your first home, odds are fairly high that you won't stay there for very long. You should be as realistic as possible, knowing that you may need to sacrifice something big (such as size or location). *The important part is determining what items you can't live without.* These items may include a garage, an easy commute or a large yard.

In this process, there are many questions that you will need to ask yourself. Although your first home—or any home that you purchase—may not be exactly what you want, you deserve to find the home that best suits you at a price you can afford. When making your "wish list" of what you want in your next home, consider these questions.

What are my needs and/or my family's needs? If you have school-aged children, you obviously will have to look at the quality of schools in a particular neighborhood. You also want to make sure that you have enough bedrooms, and you may also need room for guests. How essential is a home office, a yard or a basement? What are your options for expanding the home if you decide to do so in the future?

Where do I want to buy? Location is often the key for most homebuyers. It can affect school choices, resale values, convenience and peace of mind. You may have a perfect location in mind, but if you don't, there are some things to consider. How far are you from schools and work? Would you spend too much time driving to work or driving your children to functions? Is the neighborhood quiet and family oriented, or urban and convenient? Do you prefer the suburbs or a more cosmopolitan setting? You need to decide what will best fit the lifestyle that you and your family prefer. Are there nearby recreational activities that are appealing and convenient? If you have medical issues, you may have to factor those into your decision as well.

How much maintenance can I handle? If you do not like to do home repairs and improvements (and especially if you would have to hire someone to do even basic maintenance), you may want to consider a new home or a condo or townhouse. Buying a home that is a "fixer-upper" will involve a lot of work—and really, any home takes some work to keep it in good running order. If you are not particularly handy, you may want a home that is as low maintenance as possible.

How long do I intend to stay in this home? The longer you intend to stay, the more important your home's appreciating in price will be. Although the home you may be inclined to buy may not have the size you would like at the time you purchase it, if it has enough room for adding on at a later date, it may still be a good candidate for your residence. Also, if you are looking for a long-term home, you may be best off spending your money on a home that needs some upgrading or expansion but is located in the best neighborhood you can afford. The likelihood is that you will have more time and money over the years to make it the home you ultimately desire. Conversely, if you anticipate that you are just going to use this purchase as a home for a limited amount of time, all you may need is a clean, move-in-ready environment.

Does my job allow for stability? Even if you hope to find a home that you want to stay in for the long term, you must consider whether your job could affect this decision. Based on the nature of your employment, you may face the reality that you will have to move within the next few years to another city or state. You must take that into consideration as you make your decision.

Types of Homes

Homes come in all shapes and sizes. There are Cape Cods, Victorians, Georgians, old and charming, contemporary and sleek, condos, cooperatives and townhouses. Deciding which home is best for you can certainly be challenging. Aside from style, several other questions may help you narrow your search to the homes that will best fit your family, your lifestyle and your budget.

First, do you need a single-story or multistory home? Both have their advantages. With a single-story home, you generally have a more open floor plan, and for some people, not having to walk up and down the stairs is important. The big bonus of a multilevel home is that you generally get more square footage for a little less money, because it takes less land to build up rather than out.

Should you buy a new(er) home or an older one? Again, there are pros and cons for both types of homes. Look at some of the differences between newer and older homes to see which will best meet your needs. (Remember, these are simply examples of what you may find—there will be older homes with these items and newer homes without them.)

Newer Homes

Pros	Cons
Modern amenities (some with warranties)	Smaller lots
Larger room sizes and higher ceilings	Closer neighbors
More counter space in the kitchen and more cabinets	Less landscaping
More windows	Sometimes lower-quality building materials and workmanship
More closet space, often with large walk-in closets	No owner-added upgrades such as draperies, extra shelving, etc.

Older Homes

Pros	Cons
Building character (molding, paneled doors, hardwood floors)	Smaller rooms

Older Homes

Pros	Cons
Can be less expensive	Less storage space
Larger lot sizes	May need more upkeep and maintenance
More privacy Owner-added extras such as window treatment, built in book cases, and so forth	Will eventually need updated kitchens, bathrooms, plumbing and air/heat (if not already updated)
Older, more established neighborhoods	

Condos and Townhouses

For many people (especially first-time buyers), a condo, cooperative or townhouse can be a great first home. In fact, in Northern Virginia, because of the price of real estate, these types of residences may very well be the only practical option for a first-time buyer—and they can be the hottest sector of the real estate market. They are usually less expensive than single-family homes, they may be located in more convenient urban areas, and they are generally relatively low maintenance. Many townhouses have a garage. They allow you to spend less on your purchase and to build up equity while living in a residence that still gives you the feel of a single-family home. There are, of course, some pros and cons to buying a condo or townhouse versus a detached home. But for many people, buying a condo or townhouse has been an excellent launching pad to both building credit and building equity toward a down payment for a single-family home.

Condos, Cooperatives and Townhouses

<u>Pros</u>	<u>Cons</u>
Less expensive per square foot	Shared walls with neighbors
More modern (most condos in Northern Virginia have been built in recent years)	May lack a garage or sufficient storage
May have amenities (pools, spas, gyms, tennis courts)	Owner is responsible for condo association dues earmarked for overall maintenance and improvement of the facilities; fees can range from $160 to $400 per month
Generally have secured/gated buildings	Less privacy (and more neighbors) than in a single-family home
Easy transition from renting	
Can make changes to the interior of the unit	
Condo association takes care of grounds maintenance and is usually responsible for repairs to roofs, decks, common halls, and the plumbing and electrical into the unit (interior plumbing and electrical issues are the owners' responsibility)	

The Interior of Your "Visualized" Home

Your wish list will have many items that you want to see in the interior of the ideal home for you and your family. A home's interior can be changed, but it can be expensive. If the inside of the home doesn't really meet your needs, you need to calculate the time and aggravation that remodeling can cost you before making any final decisions on buying the home. Below are some things to look at when looking at the interior of a potential home.

- How many bedrooms? Do you have (or plan on having) children—or more children? Do you have frequent guests? Do you need a home office?

- How many bathrooms? You usually need more than one bathroom if more than two people permanently live in a home. Older homes may only have one bathroom. If this is the case, be sure you understand what it would take (or if it is possible) to put in another bath. Homes with one bathroom are hard to resell.

- Is the kitchen size adequate for your needs? How much room is there for a table? Are the appliances up to date? Is there enough counter and cabinet space? Kitchens are the most expensive rooms to remodel. Think carefully before buying a home in which you may need to upgrade everything in the kitchen. Will you be able to live without a kitchen during a lengthy remodeling?

- Is there enough storage space? Check the garage, attic, basement and closets to see if there is enough room for all of your possessions. (This may not be a major issue: it may simply be time to go through your stuff and purge!)

- How new are the windows, roof, plumbing and electrical? The newer these items are, the better. All of these usually need to be replaced at one point or another, and they can be very costly. Do you want to be the one footing the bill? Old windows can provide very poor insulation and create extremely high energy bills; plumbing problems can seem like a never-ending nightmare. A good inspector can give you a better idea about these systems, but they should never be overlooked when making your final decision.

- Finally, are there extra items that you can't live without? Some people might be sold on a house simply because of a pool, spa, fireplace, hardwood floors, moldings or electronic systems.

5

REAL ESTATE AND THE INTERNET

You've thoroughly analyzed your financial situation. You've made the decision to buy your first home or sell your existing home and buy another. You've "visualized" what that future residence will be like, and made a detailed list of "must have" items and "nice to have" items. What is the next step? One of the first tools anyone in this situation will turn to now is the Internet. In today's real estate market, being technologically savvy is essential. Whether you're researching homes on the market or having your agent create a virtual tour of the home you have listed for sale, technology has dramatically changed the face of today's real estate transactions. The Internet has made buying and selling homes smarter and easier. Today, nearly all Americans have Internet access—through work, home or the local library—and it offers a great starting point for your home search.

When I became an agent many years ago, the functions of an agent were quite simple and straightforward. Each week, every agent would receive a set of Multiple

Listing Cards. Each of these 3-by-5 cards had a tiny picture of a home that was listed for sale in the areas in which the agent specialized. The card also provided some basic information on the home: address, square footage, size of the lot, number of rooms and so on. Agents organized these cards in shoeboxes, and those boxes were our "database" for assisting our clients. The "menu" of home financing was also quite simple, mainly consisting of 30-year mortgages at a fixed rate. Also available were Veterans Administration (VA) and Federal Housing Administration (FHA) loans with lower down payments. As my mother used to say, "Lordy, how times change." The Internet has transformed the work of agents, home buyers and sellers to an amazing extent.

Before I describe many of the ways in which the Internet can be a valuable tool in your search for a home, let me point out its limitations. Many of us have used the Internet for financial transactions ranging from purchasing airline tickets to buying books from Amazon. Millions of Americans buy and sell items on eBay. In e-commerce, on a much larger scale, major corporations spend untold amounts of money as they buy commodities and other commercial goods over the Internet every day.

But buying a home is so personal, so central to the financial lives of most individuals and families, so important to the quality of life and, finally, so complicated a transaction that the Internet should be a valuable complementary tool—a "research assistant," if you will—but not the center of your search. As I spell out below, the Internet can provide much vital information to guide you in the home-buying experience. It cannot process that information for you, however. Although you can see homes and maps and read lots of data about communities on the web, you have to process that information internally by going to see the home and the neighborhood and having an experienced professional advise you.

Internet Real Estate Research

There is an enormous wealth of information available on the web about the neighborhood, city and county to which any prospective purchaser is planning a move. A variety of sites can give you the population, crime statistics, median income and even local shopping availability and recreation opportunities in any community. Here are some sites to consider.

- *www.census.gov*: This is the federal government Census Bureau's website.

- *www.northernVirginia.com* offers a wealth of information for the region.

See Appendix B for additional Internet sites on local government, public and private schools, transportation and shopping guides.

In addition to these readily available sites, my real estate team subscribes to an Internet program called eNeighborhoods, which updates neighborhood statistics on a monthly basis for Northern Virginia and throughout the United States. (If any reader has an interest in receiving data from this program, please contact me.) You should narrow down your search to a few specific neighborhoods. Perhaps you are from the neighborhood or are already familiar with its schools and amenities. If not, you can research the neighborhood to find out if it will fit your lifestyle.

Lastly, drive around the neighborhood. This is especially important if you have already found a property in which you are interested. Do the neighbors keep up their properties? Is it mostly residential? How close is it to commercial areas? These issues are almost as important as finding a home you want to buy.

In doing your research, I recommend you also use the local newspapers. Each jurisdiction in Northern Virginia has a local newspaper—the *McLean Gazette*, the *Reston Times* and so forth—which will help to give you a "feel" for that local community. The major regional newspapers are also important sources of real estate information. *The Washington Post* has a fine real estate section which is published each Saturday, and *The Washington Times* has an excellent supplement each Friday—The Home Guide. Additionally, each of these papers has frequent articles on local real estate trends.

Real Estate Websites

Aside from the resources on the Internet for general information on various jurisdictions, many websites can provide very specific and useful data on home hunting. If you are buying a home, you can preview multiple properties on your computer from the comfort of your own home in a fraction of the time it would take to drive by and see the homes in person. This is especially important if you are relocating to Northern Virginia from another state.

You can start your search by using *www.callteamworks.com* to find homes that are currently on the market. Another useful site—*www.LongandFoster.com*—can help you research homes in Northern Virginia and many other states in the mid-Atlantic region.

The Internet search engine *www.google.com* can help you locate real estate websites specializing in the neighborhood or area in which you are especially interested. Look for websites that provide you with multiple search parameters. Start by being as specific as possible regarding the home that will best meet your needs.

Good real estate websites also provide information on schools, neighborhoods, loans and alternative housing options, as well as up-to-date listings available in the specific area of Northern Virginia where you are considering a home purchase. The main purpose of searching on the Internet is to see what kinds of homes are on the market in the area that interests you.

- Look for a website that lets you choose a broad range of parameters from which to narrow your search. Although you may want to see the widest range of homes at first, as you refine your search, you should be very specific and practical regarding the home that will best meet your needs.

- Many websites require you to sign in and will offer free "membership." Don't be discouraged by this option. By signing up, you may be contacted by a representative. (This free membership means that the Do Not Call list regulations do not apply.) If you are getting serious about buying, and if it is a seller's market (one in which homes are going quickly), learning early about a new listing can be financially rewarding.

- Many websites are owned by individual real estate agents. Therefore, you should look for their credentials on the website and maybe even some references. My website is called *www.callteamworks.com*.

My real estate team also has access to a special software program referred to as SOAR Solutions. Many of my clients have found SOAR very beneficial. Here is how it works. After extensive discussions, I enter the criteria the clients present me—criteria that describe the type of residence they are interested in purchasing. The main factors I enter into this software program are the style of the desired home, the price of that home and its location. The SOAR program can then alert clients to any residence that comes on the market and meets the criteria they have identified. Clients can receive a wide range of information or a very specific database. In other words, the SOAR program can forward daily data on specific types of homes within a city, subdivision or neighborhood, or it can offer updated general information, such as price ranges of different types of homes in a specific zip code. The client will be emailed as agents and brokers enter information into the MLS (Multiple Listing Service) program. Depending on the client's preference, the frequency of the emails can vary: clients can receive emails twice a day if they are serious and need to purchase a home quickly, or the messages can come at a more leisurely pace.

In a dynamic, fast-moving market such as Northern Virginia, the instant information provided by the SOAR program gives you an edge when you are purchasing a home. For example, I recently had clients who, for a variety of reasons, had their sights set on a rambler-style home in a certain subdivision. There were very few models of this home in that area. The clients were very motivated, and the SOAR program was a natural for them: it gave them instant and current information.

Home sellers can also benefit from the SOAR program. Let us say you are quite certain that you will move in a year or so. The profile of your home—"Four bedrooms, two and a half baths, colonial, half-acre, treed lot"—can be entered into the SOAR program, and you will receive periodic updates on what homes similar to yours are worth, thus making you better informed when it comes time for you to sell your home.

Virtual Tours

Another wonderful aspect of technology in real estate is the availability of virtual tours. You can see a picture of a house without having to drive by, but imagine getting a full tour without ever having to open a door! Technology really has made the home-buying process more convenient. But don't forget that you are simply viewing images on the Internet. I would never recommend making an offer before you have physically seen a home. The Internet photos and virtual tours will not show the major highway behind the house, the nearby power lines, or the less attractive parts of the house that were not videotaped.

About a year ago, I assisted one of my sons and his wife in their purchase of a home in Richmond, Virginia. They had their own agent, who specialized in the area, but I gave them some assistance in their search as well. They had focused on a neighborhood in Henrico County, just across the Richmond city line. The neighborhood had homes built many years ago, and it was very desirable—well located, with attractive properties. The market was also hot, as interest rates were at the lowest they had been in decades, the local economy was strong, and home prices were accelerating rapidly. Listings were selling as quickly as they appeared on the market.

An attractive home with many strong attributes—solid plaster walls, beautifully landscaped, lots of square footage and an awesome kitchen—became available. When we took our first look at the home, it seemed that there was just one major downside: as the home was basically built into a hill, the large backyard was very steep. We talked to the owners, who mentioned they had lived there for over 20 years. They had raised their children in the home and raved about the home and the neighborhood. As we walked through the home, however, it became obvious that in the rear of the first floor there was a noticeable "basement" odor. Because of the steepness of the lot, a large portion of the back of the first floor abutted the ground, and there were only small oblong windows near the top of the wall. The basement itself had a strong musty odor.

My son's agent was able to check on the background of the home by talking to other neighbors and agents who were familiar with the neighborhood. Sure enough, the home was known in the immediate neighborhood as a home with "odor issues." We would never have known this from a "virtual tour"!

In short, be aware of the limitations of researching homes on the Internet. Never—I repeat, never—buy a home sight unseen, no matter how confident you are in your computer/research skills.

(Note: Another useful aspect of the Internet in the purchase of a home is searching for a mortgage. I have included my views on this in Chapter 8.)

6

Finding a Good Realtor®

You have made a firm decision: you are ready to buy a home in Northern Virginia. Having read the first five chapters of this book, you have educated yourself on the basics (or given yourself a refresher course on the basics) and have already done some fairly extensive research on potential neighborhoods and the type of home you desire. What is the next step? From my perspective, you should next find a Realtor® in whom you have confidence. When I say "Realtor®," I am talking about a member of the National Association of REALTORS® (NAR). All members of NAR must know, understand and subscribe to NARs professional code of ethics. They represent you with a high industry standard and are held accountable to that standard.

How should you go about selecting a Realtor® or an agent? The first place to start, when you seek the assistance of any professional, is with recommendations from family members, friends or colleagues. Remember to ask *why* they like the individual. You may be looking for a different type of agent than the one they recommend. Perhaps they like an agent because they have an aggressive style, for example, while you may be looking for an easy-to-talk-to person who will gently guide you through the process.

You can also ask the manager of a real estate office in an area that you are considering for a referral. That person may be able to identify the best real estate agent for your special needs, one who knows the neighborhood in which you are interested. The manager wants you to succeed in your future transaction and will give you good advice. Before you hire an agent, though, make sure that you meet that person, question them and then decide if that representative is right for you. Taking the time to make the right decision up front can save you the hassle of looking for new representation in the middle of the buying process.

As you look for an agent you should seek one who is organized, knowledgeable, experienced and fully committed to helping you achieve your real estate objectives. They need to know the marketplace, understand the details of the forms used for each step of the home buying/listing transaction and be readily available for you if you have any questions along the way. Many work as part of a small team. Whether the agent works with other agents in the office who can help when needed, has a support staff or is part of a team of agents, having an agent who is part of a team ensures that someone is always available when you need a question answered or a phone call returned.

You want a successful agent familiar with your neighborhood. It may seem basic, but you should feel comfortable asking how many buyers they have worked with in the last year, or how many houses they have sold. Make sure that the agent is both dedicated to the profession and able to make successful transactions. If they are new to the business, make sure that they have had some business experience prior to practicing real estate and have been well trained. They must be able to utilize the latest technology and be Internet savvy and comfortable with the wide variety of computer programs that can facilitate the home-buying process. An agent with technological know-how can save you many hours of needless drive-bys and open houses.

You want to ensure that your agent is well connected. Does the agent network within the local real estate community or belong to local real estate organizations? Have they been in business for a reasonably long period of time? If not, does the agent work for a broker who has these useful connections?

Other Tips on Choosing an Agent

Hire a member of the National Association of REALTORS® to ensure that your agent is held to the highest industry standards.

If you enter into an agency relationship (such as hiring someone to act as a buyer's agent), make sure that you receive a disclosure that clearly outlines the agent's responsibilities in the transaction. On the other hand, if you don't enter into an agency agreement, do understand the level of representation that you are receiving. Your agent is not legally representing you unless you have entered into some kind of agreement. Make sure that you know the terms of that agreement.

Find out if your representative is an agent, an associate broker, or a broker. Ask your agent, too, about what additional certification they have received beyond the basic courses. You will want an agent who is current on the constantly changing technical aspects of the market—which usually means that the agent has taken advanced classes.

Inquire about the agent's marketing skills. Although an agent's marketing and networking skills may seem to be more important to sellers, they can also be invaluable to you as a buyer. If you are looking to buy a home in a tough seller's market, your agent's learning about that perfect listing first—before other brokers—can make all the difference. Avoiding bidding wars and having the opportunity to make an offer before the public becomes aware of a house for sale could get you the home you've been seeking.

You need someone who can help you navigate the technical waters of finding the home you want and can close the transaction after you locate that residence. Why do I say that? For a very simple reason: purchasing or selling a home can be a minefield.

As you think about buying a particular home, you should ask yourself innumerable questions:

- Is the property I'm interested in worth its asking price?

- How do I determine what the proper price is?

- Who is a reliable home inspector, one who will honestly determine whether there are any defects in my prospective new home?

- Which school district is my potential residence in, and how do the schools rank, locally or nationally? (Even if you have no children, the quality of schools in your area can be important if you decide to sell your home in the future.)

- What are the zoning ordinances in the immediate neighborhood?

- Might major commercial development occur nearby, affecting my property values?

- Does the county or state have any road-building plans in the area?

- Is the floodplain designated just beyond my back-yard zoned "in perpetuity" or "temporarily"?

- Which condo costs are deductible?

In addition to advising on these types of issues, your agent can also assist you on all of the legal contracts, addenda, appropriate federal and state disclosures and forms that you will sign when you buy a home. Many buyers feel so excited about finding a home that, in the absence of the counsel of an agent, they might just sign any contract offer without fully understanding all the terms of a legally binding contract.

When you hire an agent, you will gain substantial benefits. First, an agent knows the value of homes in any particular marketplace. Also, in a fast seller's market, an agent may have knowledge of homes coming on the market that have not yet been entered into a Multiple Listing Services (MLS). Having the broadest selection of homes and (most important) finding out about these listings at the earliest possible moment will give you an invaluable edge in your search. An agent has been trained to guide you in making a sound financial decision, to ensure that you are treated fairly and to protect your legal interests in buying or selling a home.

Realtor® Designations

You want an agent who continues their education. Laws and standards continually change, and your agent should be aware of these changes in order to provide you with the best and most current information and advice. Finding an agent with some of the designations listed below can help you determine the agent's level of knowledge.

GRI—(Graduate REALTORS® Institute)—This designation is given after the agent completes approximately 80 hours of advanced training after becoming licensed. Many professionals will have completed this training.

CRS—(Certified Residential Specialist)—This designation denotes the completion of numerous advanced courses on a variety of topics. In order to hold this designation, a Realtor® must be willing to put in a great deal of time and effort toward furthering his or her education. Becoming a graduate also entitles the Realtor® to continued access to new and emerging real estate information. Before receiving this designation, an agent must have sold a certain number of homes.

e-PRO—An e-PRO is a Realtor®who has successfully completed the e-PRO training program for real estate professionals. Endorsed by the National Association of REALTORS®, the e-PRO course teaches professionals the "nuts and bolts" of working with real estate websites, email, online tools such as home tours, instant access to neighborhood data, email notification of just-listed homes, and referral networks.

SRES—(Seniors Real Estate Specialist)—These Realtors® are qualified to address the special needs and concerns of older citizens. Since 1998, the Senior Advantage Real Estate Council® (SAREC®) has offered a specific designation, SRES®, to identify those members who have successfully completed its educational program along with other prerequisites. By earning the SRES designation, your Realtor® has demonstrated the requisite knowledge and expertise to counsel senior clients through major financial and lifestyle transitions involved in relocating, refinancing or selling a family home.

ABR—(Accredited Buyer Representative)—The ABR designation shows an agent's dedication to enhancing their skills in buyer representation. It also proves the agent's proficiency in meeting the special needs of buyers.

Agency

When you enter into a relationship with an agent, it is important to understand that person's role in the transaction and to know your exact level of representation. In the business, this is typically referred to as "agency relationships." Agency disclosures are an important component of the real estate purchasing and selling process. Virginia law requires agents to disclose to all parties who they represent. This puts everyone on a level playing field. We Realtors® hold our fiduciary responsibilities to our clients at the highest level, yet we also have an ethical requirement (National Association of Realtors® code of ethics, which we all take an oath to abide by) to treat all parties of every transaction fairly and honestly. This is known as the *law of agency* and every state has similar requirements. Agency contracts are complicated, but you should familiarize yourself with the various kinds of representation available to you.

I should start by defining the term "agency." An agency relationship is formed when you hire someone to represent your interests in a particular transaction. In Northern Virginia, when someone acts as an agent for a client, that agent assumes certain obligations on behalf of the client. Let me put it another way. An agency relationship can be formed between a principal (that is, a client, who is buying or selling a home) and an agent who will represent the principal. Look at the principal as the "body." The agent is like an "arm" of that "body," an extension of the principal. An arm will do no harm to the body, and an agent will do no harm to the principal. The arm, in fact, performs at the will of the body. The principal makes all final decisions. The agent acts solely to benefit the principal. It is important to understand that the principal can hire and fire an agent, but an agent can also choose not to represent a principal. An agent is not obligated to represent every wish of a principal. An agent *must* end an agency relationship if a principal expects an agent to act in a manner that violates the Professional Realtor® code of ethics.

Homebuyers choose to use an agent (rather than representing themselves) for many reasons. The primary reason is that an agent has extensive knowledge, skills and experience in a particular field. If you need legal help, you immediately consult an attorney. Professionals are better educated in their specific areas of expertise, and thus are better equipped to handle particular transactions.

Buyer's Agent

A buyer's agent is someone who agrees to fulfill certain duties to the buyer by entering into an agency relationship with him or her. If you are buying a home, this relationship offers many advantages. You want to make sure that your interests are protected throughout the transaction, and you can best achieve that by hiring someone to act as your sole representative.

Having a buyer's agent represent you throughout a purchase is like having a sophisticated negotiator on your side. There is no difference in compensation between hiring a sales agent or hiring a buyer's agent. Thus, you should certainly get the best representation and protection.

Buyer agency emerged in the 1980s as a way for agents to provide better service to their clients. Agency laws had, in the past, generally offered many protections to sellers while leaving buyers to their own devices. Most people believed—and laws were often written to reflect this—that because the seller was paying the only commission on the transaction, that person's interests should be paramount. Unfortunately, at times, this system left buyers without adequate representation.

In response to this dilemma, agents and homebuyers across the country began to lobby for legislation to ensure that buyers had equal access to quality representation. These agency laws gave buyers access to individual representation without the potential problem of the agent having fiduciary duties to the seller. This is known as "sub-agency." Some of the duties of a buyer's agent include informing prospective homebuyers of anything wrong with a house and providing information about the neighborhood and the real estate transaction itself. A buyer's agent has no fiduciary duties to the seller. In fact, a buyer's agent is legally obligated both to keep your information confidential and to represent only *your* interests in the transaction.

A buyer's agent is better educated and prepared to research a wide selection of properties to ensure that you make a good purchase. The agent looks at the total purchasing process so that your best interests are represented as you select a house that meets your needs in regard to location, price and style.

Another benefit of hiring a buyer's agent is assistance in a competitive seller's market. Without question, the real estate market in the last few years has undergone a tremendous surge in home buying. Low interest rates and loan programs that are easy to qualify for have created a highly competitive market for homebuyers. Having a buyer's agent can be very useful if you are trying to outbid other buyers in a multiple-offer scenario. An agent can help you structure an offer in such a way that it will get more attention—for example, with better terms, fewer contingencies or a price that meets both your needs and those of the seller.

A buyer's agent can also be useful as a referral source for inspectors and mortgage lenders. Buyer's agents have access to the names of qualified people that work to make sure that you are well represented in all aspects of a real estate transaction. Once again, the buyer's agent examines the entire transaction and acts as your personal representative from the first interview to the final closing date.

In short, when you are buying a house in Northern Virginia, you may choose to work with a buyer's agent. You would sign a contract with the agent agreeing to work with them exclusively for a limited period of time. In return, the agent would agree to act on your behalf, which entails the following legal responsibilities:

- To exercise reasonable care and diligence;

- To deal honestly and in good faith;

- To present all written offers, written notices and other written communications to and from the parties in a timely manner without regard to whether the property is subject to a contract for sale or the buyer is already a party to a contract to purchase;

- To disclose material facts known by the buyer's agent and not apparent or readily ascertainable to a party;

- To account in a timely manner for money and property received from or on behalf of the buyer;

- To be loyal to the buyer by not taking action that is adverse or detrimental to the buyer's interest in a transaction;

- To disclose in a timely manner to the buyer any conflict of interest, existing or contemplated;

- To advise the buyer to seek expert advice on matters related to the transaction that are beyond the agent's expertise;

- To maintain confidential information from or about the buyer except under subpoena or court order, even after termination of the agency relationship; and

- Unless agreed otherwise in writing, to make a continuous, good faith effort to find property for the buyer, except that a buyer's agent is not required to seek additional properties for the buyer while the buyer is subject to a contract for purchase.

(Note, though, that a buyer's agent *may* show properties in which you are interested to other prospective buyers without breaching an affirmative duty to you. It is also important to remember that a buyer's agent does not represent the seller, even if the buyer's agent receives compensation, either in full or in part, from the seller or through the seller's agent.)

1

How Much Home Can You Afford and What's the Right Mortgage for You?

In this chapter, I spell out the financial aspects of home buying so you can be confident that you are making wise decisions. The more you know about mortgages, the better decisions you will make, and that in turn will help make your experience of purchasing a home as smooth as possible. The mortgage process is a central link in the chain of purchasing real estate. Understanding this process can simplify the entire home-buying experience and set you on a path that will help you achieve your long-term financial objectives.

Statistics prove that over the long term, owning a home costs less than renting. That's the good news. The more challenging news is that prices for homes in Northern Virginia have risen rapidly. Nevertheless, I'm convinced that you can find a home and obtain a mortgage that meets your needs. I find it gratifying to see my clients move from a rental into a purchased property, or move from their present home into their "dream home." Owning real estate in Northern Virginia still remains within most people's reach. The information in this chapter will set you on the path to fulfilling your homeownership goals. Let's explore how *you* can make your dream come true.

The Real Cost of Your Home

Almost no one is in a financial position to buy a home solely with cash. (Actually, for a variety of reasons, you might not want to pay all cash even if you were in a position to do so.) How do you get the money you need? Well, it's simple; you take out a mortgage.

What if all you know about mortgages is from ads on the TV or the Internet, and quite frankly, you're somewhat confused? How do you go about getting a mortgage, especially one that's right for you? I'll be answering these questions as we move through this chapter. The information included has been reviewed by experienced loan officers whom I have dealt with over the years.

So what exactly is a mortgage, and what are you getting yourself into? Technically speaking, a mortgage is simply the pledging of property as security for the repayment of a loan. This term, however, is most often used to refer to the loan itself. (Note: In Northern Virginia, mortgages are technically "deed of trust notes".) Choosing the right mortgage is a critical phase of your home purchase. One of the most common mistakes the average homebuyer makes is thinking that the home itself is the most expensive purchase. In reality, it's almost always the mortgage, because of the extensive interest you will pay over the life of the loan. (The tax deductibility of the interest paid on the mortgage loan partially compensates for that expense.)

The first step in considering a mortgage is to look at your overall finances and figure out how much of a monthly mortgage payment you can realistically and comfortably afford. Your monthly mortgage payment must be equal to or less than what your lender determines. This is the process of being "qualified" for a loan, which should be done before you ever look at a home to purchase.

Several variables determine the level of mortgage payment for which you qualify. The major variables include your income; the size of the down payment (obviously, the larger the down payment, the more the lender is protected, which means that your qualifying is easier); your credit worthiness (which takes car loans and credit card debt into account); and your work history. You can make some "back of the envelope" calculations to estimate, roughly, the mortgage payment for which you may qualify. First, get the average current interest rate for the type of mortgage in which you are interested. Take your gross monthly income (and your spouse's, if applicable) and multiply it by .40. Finally, subtract your long-term monthly debts—for instance, car loans, personal loans, credit card loans and alimony. Some lenders will qualify you by using higher ratios to income—i.e., more generous terms—but be very cautious if you are considering such a mortgage.

Types of Mortgages

What you can afford monthly is one issue. Finding the right mortgage to fit into that budget is a whole other ball game. After you've thought through and calculated how much you can afford for a monthly mortgage payment, you must focus on the issue of what type of mortgage would be best for your situation. Obviously, you need a type of loan that meets both your near-term budget realities and your long-term financial goals.

If you plan to live in your property for the long term, you may want to get a 30-year fixed-rate mortgage. Conversely, if you are buying a starter home, then a five-year adjustable-rate mortgage is probably the right approach. If your planned retirement is within 10 or 15 years, you may want to get a 15-year loan. Although your monthly payments would be somewhat higher with this mortgage (though not as high as you might think), you would own your property much sooner, and you could make your retirement coincide with having no mortgage payment. Others may find it important to minimize their monthly expenses and, therefore, might choose an interest-only mortgage.

Not all lenders offer the same types of loans, so knowing what type of mortgage suits you best is key. I want to emphasize that *the decision you make on which type of mortgage to take out is extremely important.* This is a time to do some serious thinking about the right balance between what you can afford as a monthly mortgage payment for a number of years and your long-term lifestyle and financial goals.

At first glance, taking out a mortgage that minimizes your monthly mortgage payment has a very strong appeal, because that frees up funds to meet other expenses. The two main avenues for a mortgage that minimizes your cost in the early years are ARMs (adjustable-rate mortgages) and "interest-only" ARMs.

When you have an ARM, you receive from the lender an initial interest rate below the current rate quoted for a 30-year fixed mortgage. For example, if the rate for a 30-year mortgage is 6 percent, the rate for a five-year ARM will typically be 5.375 percent *for the first five years of the loan.* So the good news is that on a mortgage of $300,000 the monthly payments would be $1,679 for the ARM versus $1,798 for the 30-year, thus saving you substantial out-of-pocket expenses during that five-year period. The bad news is that at the end of the five years, the lender has the option to increase the rate of your mortgage. The extent of the increase depends on the parameters set forth in the original mortgage.

As its name clearly indicates, the "interest-only ARM" loan is a variant of the ARM, one that offers even lower monthly payments, because none of your monthly payment goes toward paying down the principal of the loan. The monthly payment on a $300,000 mortgage for this type of loan would be $1,375 per month. However, at the end of the five years, the amount you owe on your $300,000 mortgage is still $300,000.

Let's take a moment to look at the 30-year mortgage vis-à-vis the 15-year mortgage. Once again, let's assume that the mortgage loan is for $300,000 and the interest rate is 6 percent. The monthly payments on the 30-year mortgage are $1,798. The monthly payments on the 15-year loan are $2,531. Notice that although the amount of time you have to pay off the mortgage is completely cut in half with the 15-year loan, the monthly payment increases by just 40 percent. Obviously, you are also paying down the principal much more rapidly with the 15-year mortgage. If you are disciplined in handling your budget, a good alternative to the 15-year mortgage is to take out a 30-year mortgage but accelerate the payment on it to 13 payments per year (or other accelerated rates) and pay it off early.

Of course, everyone's personal finances, time in life, career outlook and long-term goals are different. A blending of these factors must be considered when you make a decision on what type of mortgage is best for you. For some, the decision can be a no-brainer. For example, if you are 20-something and have a limited budget but feel very strongly that you want to get started in real estate ownership, an ARM or interest-only ARM is the way to go. Conversely, if you are middle aged, looking forward to a reasonably early retirement and always wanted to own "your little piece of the planet," having a 15-year mortgage may be preferable. All kinds of circumstances can have an impact on this decision. For example, if you are set to receive the proceeds of a trust fund or some sort of inheritance at a certain set date, that can affect the type of mortgage that may best meet your needs. If you are a government worker with reasonable assurances of a steadily increasing income, you may prefer a fixed-rate loan. If you are in the private sector, paid on a commission basis and often experience wide swings in annual income, an ARM or "interest-only ARM" may be appealing.

Conforming and Nonconforming Mortgages

The vast majority of mortgages are resold in the so-called "secondary market." This usually involves the originator of the mortgage selling it to Fannie Mae (Federal National Mortgage Association) or Freddie Mac (Federal Home Loan Mortgage Corporation). Conforming loans are mortgages that meet the qualifications to be purchased by Fannie Mae or Freddie Mac. Conforming loans cannot be above a certain ceiling, which, however, is periodically revised upward. Because of their liquidity in the secondary market, conforming loans will typically offer better terms to the borrower.

Nonconforming loans, which don't meet the qualifications to be purchased by Fannie Mae or Freddie Mac, are held in the portfolios of banks, savings and loans and other institutions. There are a wide variety of nonconforming loans, and a number of niche mortgage programs exist that fit the special mortgage needs of certain buyers.

Points and Truth-in-Lending

My clients ask two questions quite frequently. What are points? What is the "Truth-in-Lending" document? The term "points" refers to either an origination fee or "discount" points. A "point" is 1 percent of the amount of the mortgage loan. The origination fee is a charge paid to the lender for processing your loan application. Typically, the maximum origination fee is 1 percent of the loan and this fee can be amortized into your loan. Taking that approach results in a slightly higher interest rate that is offset by lower costs up-front. Discount points are fees that you can pay if you want a lower interest rate.

A Truth-in-Lending statement is a document, required by federal law, which must be given to buyers when they are "locking in" a loan. All information on the actual costs of the mortgage is listed on this statement. Be sure that you review this document prior to committing to the interest rate of your potential loan. The most important number to check is the APR–Annual Percentage Rate. The APR is the cost of a mortgage stated as a yearly rate and includes items such as interest, mortgage insurance and, if applicable, loan origination fees and discount points.

Conclusion

In sum, you have to balance your desires and commitment to living in your "dream home" against how that goal affects your overall budget. For example, you may be approved for a certain loan amount based on your income and assets. The monthly payment on that mortgage that you can technically afford, however, may not be appropriate given your broader financial priorities and necessities—for example, education costs for children, vacations or retirement contributions. From my perspective, living in a home that is so expensive that your other financial and lifestyle goals go unmet is not wise.

As you can see, there are so many variables in the loan qualification process; it is now time to discuss finding the right type of lender to assist you. It may take you a little effort to find the right lender, but that individual is out there just waiting to approve your loan.

8

How to Find a Good Lender

Choosing the right mortgage lender is like selecting any other business professional. When you take the advice of your stockbroker, you do so because you believe that the broker deserves your trust, and you feel confident that person will give you sound advice on how to invest your money wisely. Look for these same qualities—honesty and competence—in a mortgage lender. Keep in mind that it's your money on the table in this transaction. *Referrals from people you trust remain the best way to find potential mortgage lenders.* Ideally, the people you ask will have recently shopped for a mortgage or can refer you to reputable people in the mortgage industry. Ask your agent, tax advisor, attorney or financial consultant for referrals. Another referral source is friends, relatives or neighbors who have bought and sold a few homes over the past number of years. You will need to do some comparison shopping, so don't be shy about asking for referrals; it will save you time and money. Whenever anyone gives you a referral, ask why they recommend that person. Don't automatically assume that lender will be the right one for you, though. You want to choose someone who is knowledgeable, provides good service and offers competitive rates and low fees—not just someone's next-door neighbor.

It is very difficult to wade through the myriad of options and regulations to determine the best mortgage for you. Mortgage lending is a specialized business with programs, rates and fees that change rapidly and vary widely. When you are ready to commit to taking out a mortgage, turning to an expert will put experience and knowledge on your side. By reading this chapter, you'll learn what types of mortgages to look for, what questions to ask potential lenders and even what information you must present to a potential lender. Your reward will be making the right decision on the largest purchase of your life.

You will need answers to many questions. Choose a lender who will take the time to explain to you the variety of loan program options available and to assist you in making the right choice among those options. You need to feel comfortable that you will work well together. You can start with these questions.

- What types of loans do they specialize in? Do they specialize in financing the types of real estate you intend to purchase?

- Do they have a local underwriting capability? This may help you get a quick answer when you ask about qualifying for a loan.

- How competitive are their rates? After comparison shopping, you'll know the answer. Be careful about a lender who quotes rates significantly lower than everyone else's. They may not deliver on the rate quoted, or the "low-rate mortgage" may have large fees or prepayment penalties attached, thus offsetting the attractiveness of the lower rate.

During your interview, pay attention to whether the loan officer openly answers your questions and discloses fees. Once you've formed your list of a few potential candidates, ask for customer references. Call the customers to ask how the lender handled their loan, using the previous questions as a guide. Ask if the lender promptly returns phone calls and answers questions correctly, produces loan documents quickly and accurately, and honors commitments. This may seem like a lot of work, but you don't want to find out that you picked the wrong lender a week before closing.

In sum, find a capable and knowledgeable lender through referrals. Look for overall good customer service. *Remember, don't just shop for the lowest quoted rate.* "Quoted" lower rates do not guarantee the lender's ability to get your loan approved. You must consider not only the interest rate but also the overall terms of the mortgage and the lender's likelihood of honoring the quotes given.

Keep your decisions logical and on track. Search for a lender who will best meet your needs. Don't necessarily get your mortgage from a local or national bank just because it handles your checking account or your car loan.

Alternative Sources for Mortgages

You have plenty of alternatives in shopping for a loan. Your options include independent mortgage brokers, banks, savings and loans, credit unions and corporations that specialize in offering mortgages through the Internet and telemarketing. Throughout the process of actually looking for a lender, keep in mind my earlier point: Your long-range mortgage interest expenses will cost more than your house. You must be very focused on getting the best possible mortgage, one that meets your requirements and objectives. In the following section, I offer brief descriptions of the various types of institutions and individuals involved in the mortgage business.

Institutional Lenders

I personally recommend using institutional lenders—banks, savings and loans, credit unions or mortgage banks—that offer local processing, underwriting and closing of mortgage loans. In many cases, this could be a large lending institution with a nationwide presence that still has the ability to process your loan at the local level.

The major reason I suggest this avenue is that when an institutional lender issues an approval letter—a letter that states they will approve a loan for you up to a certain level—the loan has already been underwritten and there is a commitment to lend the money. In the Northern Virginia real estate market, having an approval letter is absolutely essential for the home-buying process (see Chapter 9). Other mortgage lenders generally do not offer this service.

Large mortgage lenders have well-trained, knowledgeable loan officers. They usually are as informed as the typical mortgage broker. They also, in many cases, can act as a broker if necessary.

Although I prefer that my clients use these types of institutions when obtaining a mortgage, the reader should be aware that you still have to do your homework when selecting which institution to use. There can be a downside if you don't select carefully. For example, many large institutions that have hundreds of branches use a central facility to process their loans. But large centralized processing centers are not an advantage, as their operations can be cumbersome. If the processor in that central facility needs more information about a loan, that person will call the loan officer, who will then call the client. If the processor doesn't approve a loan, the loan officer can repackage the loan for reconsideration. Look for a "local" or "in house" underwriting and closing department. In this scenario, your loan officer has direct communications with the decision makers. This would be the best situation, because your loan officer retains a certain amount of control.

The loan officers of most companies are usually paid a percentage of the mortgage loan amount, but some are salaried employees. If they are salaried employees, they have little flexibility to negotiate rates; if they are commissioned, they have much more latitude. Other expenses, such as underwriting or document fees, can be waived, so check with the manager. Because most financial corporations are well known, you probably don't need to delve into their history. Do make an appointment to meet the loan officer in person, though. Be sure to ask the general questions noted earlier as well as the questions listed below.

- How does the loan officer receive compensation?

- If it's by commission, ask the loan officer if the company offers bonuses for certain types of loans. (For example, the loan officer may get a higher commission by selling a loan with a prepayment penalty.)

- If the loan officer receives a bonus for certain loans, ask which ones. Make sure the loan officer understands that you will not consider any of those programs.

Independent Mortgage Brokers

An independent mortgage broker does not work for any specific bank or lending institution. They are an independent contractor who will be able to place your mortgage application with a wide variety of corporations. A good independent mortgage broker can help you navigate the sea of confusion, counsel you on loans from different "wholesale lenders" and save you time and energy. Since independent brokers are not directly employed by banks or corporations who have money to lend, they have more choices of loans, especially for first-time buyers. They can take advantage of rates offered by out-of-state banks, for example. A bank must be licensed to operate in a state, but they can work through a mortgage broker as a wholesaler, which gives independent brokers broader options. Independent brokers generally get paid by receiving a commission from the bank that accepts your loan—and by you, through possible points charged on your loan amount. Information and facts that would take the borrower hours to research are at the mortgage broker's fingertips and are a part of his or her everyday world. A good broker will be intimately familiar with the dynamics of the mortgage loan market. That person can advise you on when to lock in a rate, whether a fixed or adjustable rate will be the best fit, and how to frame or package your information so that reputable lenders will likely approve your application. Independent mortgage brokers shop loans among many wholesale lenders, so they know which lenders specialize in what the client wants, and they won't waste time trying to approve your loan with the wrong lender.

Having made those positive points, I should quickly add that there could be a number of drawbacks involved in dealing with an independent mortgage broker. An important issue is the time it takes to identify that good independent broker. You have to check referral sources thoroughly. Many brokers come into the mortgage business during a "boom" and are gone in the "bust." If you decide to go with an independent broker for your mortgage needs, make certain that person has been in the business for a long time and can provide verifiable customer service.

Another downside to using independent brokers is that they have no "in-house" underwriting (the process that actually approves your loan). They are also not in charge of the preparation of documents needed for the final settlement, nor are they accountable for the issuance of approval or pre-approval letters, which are so important in the negotiation process of buying a home. Although a good independent broker will work hard to get the client's loan approved, the decision to approve or reject an application does not lie with that broker directly. Finally, they are last in line when it is time to get your loan underwritten or closed. A bank or similar institutional lender will always give its own branch retail sites highest priority. Only after those sites are accommodated will the bank review and work on "brokered loans." In a fast-paced environment, brokered loans don't always close on time and often have additional mark-up charges that can vary from 1 to 3 percent of the loan amount.

Some wholesale lenders push certain loans to independent brokers and pay them a higher commission for selling those loans. Finding a lender you can communicate with can help relieve you of this worry. If you decide to use an independent mortgage broker, besides the questions raised earlier, remember to ask these additional questions.

- What is the mortgage broker's experience, education and expertise?

- How many loans has the broker funded in the last year? How many were approved or denied? Choose a lender with a high approval rate; that person knows how to solve problems and take care of a client.

- How long does it take to process a typical loan?

- How much time will it take for the loan to be "underwritten" so you can get a final approval?

- How is the broker compensated? Even if the person is not legally obligated to tell you, they have no reason to skip the answer because the final loan document will disclose the broker's compensation. All of your questions need satisfactory answers.

Telemarketers

In your search for a lender, you will find plenty of candidates. I urge you to exercise caution with companies that use call centers to market their mortgages. These companies may advertise their phone centers or may call you at home to try to sell you a loan. They have little accountability, and their employees usually have limited knowledge. They often are not skilled in the nuances of mortgage approval. Do you want such an important expenditure to be handled by someone who is not a trained professional?

Employees of call centers may claim that they can get anyone approved for a loan, but at what price? People have been known to pay considerably more in closing costs and interest rates on a mortgage with some of these companies. This could mean tens of thousands of your hard-earned dollars. In general, it is in your best interest to avoid such marketing ploys and consider some of the other alternatives discussed above.

Finding a Loan on the Internet

Before the Internet, financial information and research materials were only available to the public during regular business hours. Now vast amounts of information are available 24 hours a day—all at the touch of a mouse. This phenomenon has taken the pressure off mortgage shopping and can help you ease into your search for the right lender and the right mortgage. As a research tool, the Internet offers tremendous opportunities to expand your knowledge about mortgages at your own pace and on your own time. Information that in the past was only available to lenders is now accessible to everyone. You have access to up-to-date rates, for instance, without calling a lender.

Undoubtedly, you would have to make a lot of calls to get the same information that you can quickly get online. Even so, I recommend caution. Today, with an innumerable number of sites about mortgages, information overload can make a confusing process even more perplexing. With so many choices, how do you find the mortgage that will best meet your needs? Again, the Internet is useful for information, but it cannot interpret that information. At the end of the day, at least from my perspective, you should take the information that you learned from the Internet to a professional you have confidence in, one who can help verify that information and interpret it in light of your specific situation.

An online lender or mortgage company may not give you full service. Some companies may require you to provide some personal information before they will give you a quote. In the early stages, when mortgage shopping first became available online, most companies using this medium focused on price as a way to attract customers. They really did not offer quality service. An incompetent lender could even cost you money.

Efficiency and timeliness can best be achieved with a personal, hands-on lender. There are many stories about lenders who use low "come-on" rates and then increase the rates just before closing on the mortgage loan. Because I only use lenders I know and whose professionalism I have confidence in, I have not had problems with any online lenders for the clients I have represented. But sitting across the settlement table in many transactions over the years, I have witnessed cases where the "other party" has had serious issues with online lenders. A lender can mislead you about rates, but it's much easier for this to happen when you're not looking the lender in the eye.

Most mortgage sites offer free listings to lenders, which makes them similar to online Yellow Pages. Some offer higher visibility listings—for instance, at the top of a section, or in a special typeface—if the lender pays a fee. To the unsuspecting buyer, these companies may seem more prestigious or somehow better than others. So how do these sites get their lenders? Is there any quality control to check that a participating lender follows through on its promises?

The reality is that there isn't a great deal of accountability with online lenders. There are no guarantees. You can try clicking on the area of the site that solicits lenders and review the site's criteria, but this doesn't mean that there aren't other means of solicitation. Ultimately, you will have to verify the facts and check on the legitimacy of the lenders.

To figure out whether securing an online mortgage is the way for you to go, let's look at a few points. In this complicated and extremely important transaction, you want to find a lender you can trust to deal honestly with you, one who knows the mortgage business. The same questions you'd ask a lender in person need to be asked of an online lender.

- In which types of loans does the lender specialize? Remember, you want a lender who has experience with the type of real estate you want to buy.

- How does the approval process work?

- How competitive are the rates? Again, please be suspicious of anyone who quotes rates significantly lower than everyone else's. As we discussed, these rates may have penalties attached—or the lender knows that you won't qualify for the lowest rate, and you will end up with a much higher rate.

- Does the lender openly answer questions and disclose fees?

- Is the lender familiar with loan, appraisal and settlement companies in your area? Every state deals with these items differently, and if the lender doesn't know how to close a loan in your state, you could be in for a major disaster—including possibly losing out on a house or having to switch lenders at the last minute. In fact, this is the most frequent complaint about online lenders. When it comes to the details, a lender in Florida may have no idea how to get an appraisal in Northern Virginia or how to work with a local escrow company. This can be a major deal killer, so make sure that the lender has offices here in Northern Virginia.

If you are convinced that you want to get a mortgage through the Internet, I would advise you to ask for the names, numbers and dates of the last few clients the lender funded. Check those references. Verify with the clients that the information the lender gave you is correct. Some considerations and questions are:

- What level of service does the lender offer?

- Does the lender have the time to answer questions and address concerns down the line?

- How much help will the lender give you?

- Does the lender simply process your application, or will the representative work to get you approved?

- Is the lender experienced enough to help you decide the best time to lock in a rate?

- What are the security and confidentiality policies of the lender? In deciding on an online lender, you will need to ask yourself if you feel comfortable sending reams of personal and financial information over the web.

One of the biggest questions (and the one that draws most people to shop for a loan online) is: Do you actually save money? There usually is not much variance in the interest rates you're offered, because they are all controlled by the same market factors. This means that the same rate online can most likely be found with a good lender that you can talk to in person and with whom you can establish a solid working relationship. Much of online mortgage advertising emphasizes rates. While rates are important, keep in mind that knowing what kind of loan you need is just as crucial.

Some online brokers may take a smaller commission for processing your loan online. Even so, you will probably want to have the comfort of knowing the person responsible for handling your confidential and important paperwork. Some sites boast that they will save you thousands of dollars, but there is no guarantee that they will follow through at crunch time. They may not deliver the prices they advertise. Also, it is essential that you are aware that online mortgage brokers can "shop your loan" through several financial institutions. These institutions will do a credit inquiry; once the credit inquiry is complete, a rate offer would theoretically be made based on your credit scores and profile. Remember, though, with multiple credit inquiries, your credit score may fall significantly. This lower score, in turn, could result in your not qualifying for a mortgage at the end of the inquiry trail even though you may have qualified for it at the beginning of the search!

The Northern Virginia area offers many excellent and established lenders with great reputations. In the final analysis, people feel most satisfied when they have dealt with a human being face-to-face, someone who will guide them and work with them through the entire loan procedure. Given the importance of this transaction, a small saving on a loan can't compensate for the accountability and personal service given by a broker you work with in person. A good mortgage broker in your area is intimately familiar with the local market and will know how to serve you.

As a tool for research during your preparation to take out a mortgage, I definitely encourage you to use the Internet. Explore rates and take stock of where you are with the type of loan you want. When it comes to applying for a loan, however, let your instincts guide you to choose a lender with whom you can form a personal relationship and whom you can trust. Most buyers want a person who cares about the outcome of the loan. The emotional factor comes into play again here. A good broker will understand the tension that can build as the client waits for loan approval—and will know how important approval and timeliness is to the client.

Take the knowledge you gain from the Internet to become better informed about your options, and use it as an adjunct to the information a broker in your area gives you. I don't suggest that you use the web to replace shopping for a mortgage in the traditional way. If you honestly think you've found a great deal online, find a reputable lender in your area and negotiate to see whether that lender will match what you've found. Most likely, having a serious, informed buyer will encourage the lender to meet your price. (If the lender cannot match the rates, I would be very suspicious of the rates quoted online.)

Don't ever forget that this is your money—and taking out a mortgage will be the largest purchase you will probably ever make. You have every right to shop around and ask questions before you hand over your money. Know which type of loan you are looking for and what lender specializes in it. Find a lender you feel comfortable with, one to whom you can talk. Make sure that your questions are answered to your satisfaction. Inform yourself of your options, and accept professional and experienced guidance; ultimately, though, you must decide what's right for you.

Mechanics of the Mortgage Application Process

At your first meeting, a lender will ask a few basic questions about your finances to determine the level of mortgage for which you are qualified. The first determination is whether or not your gross income can support your mortgage payment. Then the lender will ask whether you have enough liquid assets to meet the upfront cash requirements for a down payment and closing costs. In some cases, a lender may require proof that you have enough assets that can be liquidated to make a few months of mortgage payments.

The first document you will need from a lender is a preapproval letter based on the verbal information you give to the lender. It is important to understand that a pre-approval letter does not legally obligate the lender to make the loan. A recent article in the *Washington Post*, "Some Preapprovals Aren't Worth the Ink They're Printed On" (*Washington Post*, July 19, 2005, F1), described the conclusions of a national survey conducted by Campbell Communications, Inc. It read in part, "The agents said 39% of all preapprovals issued by Internet-based lenders are faulty or invalid." Other types of lenders also had problems with a percentage of their preapproval letters.

Therefore it is important to take the next step in which the lender verifies your employment, assets and liabilities before giving you a formal approval letter for a mortgage. It is essential that the data you provide to the lender is reviewed and approved by an underwriter. In a dynamic real estate market like Northern Virginia, an approval letter is absolutely essential if you are attempting to purchase a home. In an environment where there may be multiple bids on a property, the seller will usually not even consider bids that are not accompanied by a valid approval letter. In other words, your bargaining position in the negotiating process is greatly strengthened by the fact that the potential seller knows that a lender has already reviewed your finances and has determined that you qualify for the purchase of the residence.

No matter which type of lender you ultimately choose to deal with, you will need to supply a number of documents at the time you apply for a loan, including the following:

- W-2 tax forms and Federal tax returns for the last two years.

- Employment history for the last two years.

- Copy of your current month's paycheck(s).

- Copy of the contract of sale (including the legal description of the property).

- Outstanding loans (including student loans), including addresses, account numbers, balances and monthly payments.

- Information on real estate you own, including loan amounts, property addresses, loan balances and monthly payments.

- Bank statements for all accounts for the last two months, including checking and savings.

- Documents that demonstrate your vested interest in stocks, bonds or other investments.

- Divorce decree, if you are paying and/or receiving alimony or child support.

- For Veteran Administration (VA) loans only: DD214 forms and a Certificate of Eligibility.

- A check for an appraisal and credit report.

This information is quite extensive. But as a loan applicant, you must keep in mind that the lender is making a major commitment to you and has the right to determine the safety of the mortgage loan.

The loan underwriter reviews your entire monthly costs for housing, including principal, interest, mortgage insurance, homeowners insurance and taxes on the property. Every property and every home buyer varies widely in terms of the purchasers qualifications and the home's overall expenses, so it is not possible to create a specific profile that precisely shows what income is needed to pay for a home.

9

Buying Your Home

Buying a home is a very rewarding experience. Having a place to call your own and decorating it in any way you like is great. Not having a landlord who can tell you what or what not to do with your property is a big plus. Moving up to your "dream home" after owning a number of lesser residences over the years is a very big deal.

However, buying a home can also cause anxiety. Buying a home is certainly an emotional purchase. Your home may be where you will get married, or raise your children, or celebrate important moments with your family and friends. Most Americans spend much of their free time at home, and that home offers a haven from the stress and worry of the outside world. Considered a vital part of the "American Dream," homeownership and its advantages have been instilled in most of us since we were children. Immense emotional gratification and a deep sense of pride accompany homeownership. Each of us wants to provide a safe, stable and comfortable place for our family to live. As noted earlier, owning real estate also acts as a powerful investment, offering tax benefits and an appreciation in value that can play a central role in your achieving long-range financial and lifestyle goals.

These feelings can easily affect how people make decisions during the complicated procedure of getting approved for a loan, finding a home and bidding on a property (and the potential disappointment of not getting approved for your loan or not getting the property you want). I can't emphasize the following point enough: *Home buying needs to be driven more by common sense and logic than by emotion.*

Be practical as you assess homes. Some are completely updated; others will need extensive modifications. Only you can determine your individual needs when it comes to home buying. If you have the time, skills or money to do major home improvement projects and you are getting a good deal, then go for it. Similarly, you should ensure that you are not overpaying for a house just because it has new carpet, appliances or various "cosmetic" changes. Compare the interiors of the homes on your "short list" and make notes on how much you think improvements may cost. That way, you will know what you are really getting for the price.

Don't forget to consider all of the pros and cons of each home. How much home do you get in one neighborhood versus another? Keep in mind what really is included with each home by maintaining a list of all the factors. Seeing multiple residences before making up your mind is essential. A good agent can show you several properties in different areas and in different price ranges so you can really make the best decision. This is true even if you only have a limited time to look. You can take digital photographs of each property and then review them on your computer later in the day.

Now let's discuss some of the key factors in bidding on a home.

Square Footage

At first glance, trying to determine the value of a residence based on square footage is a simple, straightforward calculation. The Federal National Mortgage Association (commonly referred to as Fannie Mae or FNMA) has set forth guidelines used by appraisers and lenders. Fannie Mae is a New York Stock Exchange company and the largest nonbank financial services company in the world. It operates pursuant to a federal charter and is the nation's largest source of financing for home mortgages. Fannie Mae's square footage guidelines basically calculate the living area in the so-called above-grade space— i.e., the above-basement levels.

In reality, using square footage to help determine the right price to offer for a home is complicated. For example, many of the newer homes in suburban Virginia have 10-foot ceilings throughout the first floor and vaulted ceilings in some rooms. If you compared the price of one of these newer homes on a square foot basis to an older home with a similar floor plan (but with the traditional eight-foot ceilings), the square footage might be identical. The higher ceilings are an important upgrade, however, adding a lot to the home's "livability" and its appeal to most potential purchasers. Those higher ceilings, of course, are not reflected in the square footage numbers.

Basements are also an important factor in the square footage calculations. My home, for example, has a walkout basement with lots of sunlight flowing through the sliding-glass doors and windows. It has a fireplace, heating, air conditioning, is wired for broadband and has a television and stereo. There are no musty basement-like odors. To me, my basement "feels" like any other floor of the house. The nearest home behind me is about a fifth of a mile away because of a floodplain on the edge of my property where there is a small creek. "Mother Nature" has taken care of the landscaping, with a hundred or so trees visible from the basement. In many ways, then, the basement level is one of the most appealing selling points and attractive features of my home. Yet, technically, in calculating the value of my home, the basement is not an above-grade floor and thus receives a different valuation per square foot.

Square footage calculations can vary, too, depending on the person doing them. There have been occasional articles about complaints made to state real estate commissions over the issue of how square footage of a residence is measured. These controversies usually involve a home being advertised for sale as having more square footage than the appraiser calculates.

Taking the square footage into your decision-making process when buying a home is a good way to include facts in your purchase and to ensure you don't rely too much on emotion. Let us say, for example, that you have narrowed down your search to two properties. One of them is newly carpeted, has great appliances and is freshly painted. The other is in a similar price range but has worn carpet, too much wallpaper in many rooms and dated appliances—but considerably more square footage. While your emotions may tell you to buy the smaller home because of its ready-to-move-in condition, factoring square footage into your decision may point you in the other direction—and that would likely be a much wiser decision in the long run. If the cosmetic changes of new carpeting, stripping wallpaper, painting and buying a refrigerator bring the larger home up to the appeal of the smaller property, you probably should strongly consider buying the larger property, all other things being equal.

You should feel comfortable with your understanding of what "formula" is used to calculate the square footage of the largest purchase of your life. In fact, it would be prudent to get a floor plan with the dimensions of each room of the home, if it is newer.

How Motivated Is the Seller?

Another crucial step in determining your offering price is to try to discern how motivated the seller is and how many other offers (or interested parties) are out there. Knowing your bargaining position is essential. For instance, you may be interested in a home that is priced at $400,000. The comps—that is, the comparable prices of similar homes recently sold in the neighborhood— confirm that it is worth $400,000. You find out during the showing that the owner is relocating to another city; their company is paying the moving costs and real estate commissions, so they may be very motivated to sell. In this case, unless there are other offers on the table, a quick closing period and fair pricing may get you the home.

The more you know about the seller's motivation, the stronger your bargaining position will be. The issue is not always price! The seller may not want to sell the home to an investor but would prefer an owner occupant as a purchaser. They may need a longer period to close on their property to help with their two-year capital-gains time line, or they may want the security offered by a larger down payment. The key is to address the seller's larger concerns. I've had clients who were prepared to move quickly and were able to get a home that was under-priced solely because the sellers were *really* ready to move. The seller wanted a quick sale, a quick closing and a prepared buyer. We came in "fitting the bill", and everyone walked away happy.

Have your Realtor®, to the extent possible, find the answers to the following questions.

- Is the home still available? If the seller has just accepted an offer, it may take a day or two for it to be updated on the MLS.

- If there is an accepted offer, are there any contingencies. If so, is the seller taking backup offers?

- If the house is available, are there any pending offers? If so, try to see if the agent is willing to discuss for how long the sellers have been receiving these offers. If an offer has not been accepted for a few days, then it may not have met the asking price or it may have contained unattractive terms or contingencies. Possibly, a clean, full-price offer may stand out.

- If the seller had accepted an offer but the house is now back on the market, ask why this happened?

- When does the seller prefer to close on the property?

- How much time does the seller need to respond? This may give you an idea of how motivated the seller is to get the deal closed.

What Price Do I Offer?

There are many factors involved in deciding what price you should offer. Your agent will look at comparable sales in the neighborhood to determine the fair market value of the house. This approach enables one to ascertain whether the asking price is below or above realistic market prices. Comps are extremely useful, though they should never be the sole factor used to determine your offering price. The best way to analyze comps is to look at the prices of similar homes in the neighborhood or similar neighborhoods. Have these other homes experienced similar price increases? Will the house appraise for the asking price? Has the house had any special features added that would differentiate it from other houses in the neighborhood? Specifically, what value was added to the home by these improvements or additions?

Do not be afraid of making a lower bid on an overpriced home. Overpriced homes generally sit for long periods of time, strengthening a buyer's bargaining position. When a home is getting a great deal of traffic but no offers, sellers realize that the price may need to be adjusted. And you can often negotiate a good price with the sellers of homes that do not show well for whatever combination of factors—tasteless wallpaper, outdated carpet, old appliances and the like. If you have the vision to see past minor aesthetic issues, you may find yourself in a position to buy a home with great potential at a reasonable price.

If you are interested in making an offer on a home, particularly in a seller's market when homes are appreciating rapidly in value, time is an important factor. This may mean that even if the house just came on the market, you and your agent should try to make sure that the seller sees your contract offer as quickly as possible. Also, attempting to get special considerations while you are negotiating on the home against several other potential buyers is an easy way to lose out on a house that you may really desire.

The Terms of Your Offer

The terms that you offer will, of course, vary depending on your particular situation. The major specific components of the contract will include:

- Date, name and address of the buyer and seller, and a legal description of the property.

- The amount of "earnest money"—money that shows you are serious about wanting to purchase the home—that will be held in an escrow account.

- Price you are offering.

- Size of the down payment as well as how the remainder of the purchase price is to be financed.

- Proposed settlement and occupancy date—and daily rent provision for "post-settlement occupancy" if the seller becomes the temporary tenant of the buyer.

- Contingencies, if any, such as home inspection, appraisal, or final closing on the sale of the buyer's present home.

- Other important provisions, including a list of items that convey with the property, a stipulation that the title must be insurable, and a determination of who is to pay various settlement costs.

If you are offering a price that you are comfortable with and you have no special circumstances, you will find that the less you ask for, the better chance you have of having an offer accepted. But this does not mean that the sellers will not listen if you need certain concessions. The offer is about much more than price. Again, terms—good or bad—often make or break the deal. Sellers generally look for the cleanest offers (those with the fewest contingencies and special terms) possible. Unless you are facing a very competitive seller's market, you can ask for the terms that you need to make the offer "fit" your requirements.

You should choose your terms based on both your needs and the information you have about the seller's needs. If you need a quick closing but know that the seller wants to close later, you could consider renting a corporate apartment for a short period of time. Or if you are only offering a small down payment, you may want to ask for nothing other than a home inspection. The bottom line is that you and your agent should fully assess your position and then use the knowledge you have obtained about the seller's needs to structure the strongest offer possible.

Consider, for example, the following before deciding on terms.

- Does the seller plan to leave the washer, dryer, refrigerator, window treatments or any other personal property? If so, you want to make sure that you request that these items stay in the offer. Unless it is in writing, any item that is not considered a "fixture" does not have to convey to the new owner.

- Likewise, are there any exclusions to the offer? For example, a permanent fixture, such as a dining room chandelier, typically conveys. However the seller may want to take it and thus present it as an exclusion from items that convey. If you are competing with other buyers, you may not want to ask for such items since that may help you succeed in the contract negotiations.

Negotiating a Purchase

Everything is negotiable, so don't be upset if the seller counters your offer. Counteroffers are quite common and remember that all counter offers must be in writing to be valid. Likewise, you can always counter a counter offer. The bottom line is that you should make an offer that you are comfortable with. If at any point during the negotiations you are unhappy with the situation, you have the absolute right to back out. Until both parties have a meeting of the minds through an offer in writing, there is no valid contract.

With your offer, you will be required to submit an "earnest money" deposit. Earnest money shows that you are serious about wanting to purchase the home and gives the seller confidence that they can take the home off the market. This money will be credited toward the purchase price at the time of closing. If you do not honor the sales contract and do not follow through with the sale, the seller may be able to keep your earnest money as well as damages. If you default on the contract, the seller has the right to sue for any damages incurred.

The actual purchase process for a home is quite detailed but very straightforward. You and your agent fill out a contract offer form, deliver it to the seller and then wait to hear if your offer has been accepted, rejected or countered with a different price, different terms or both. The complicated part is strategizing with your agent to determine the price and terms of your offer and presenting that offer clearly and efficiently.

10

GETTING FROM THE CONTRACT TO CLOSING

Whether you are buying or selling a home, the hardest part is the "getting from contract to closing" time frame, when serious problems often arise. During this period, any contingencies in the contract must be satisfactorily resolved, and the home inspection takes place. Here is where "show-stopper" issues may suddenly appear. The complicated and very technical aspects of the overall transaction—including the closing—will occur at this stage, and as they say, "it ain't over until it's over." In short, if you were taking Maalox because of the stress of keeping your house immaculate during the time you had it listed for sale, and you were further stressed over the details of buying your next home—don't throw the Maalox out once you have a contract on your current home and you've presented a contract on your next home. The Maalox-free days will come *after* the closings.

Thus far, I have tried to avoid technical jargon. I hope that this book has provided you with plenty of useful information and insight. In the world of real estate transactions, however, there is no choice at times but to discuss issues by using technical terms and detailed descriptions of the process. Considering that the purchase or sale of your home is one of the largest financial transactions of your life, there should be nothing surprising about that. Still, I apologize for reverting to "technospeak" in portions of this chapter to describe the contract, the events that occur in the aftermath of the contract and the "closing" process.

The Contract

According to *West's Business Law* (Clarkson, Miller, Jentz and Cross, New York: West Publishing Company, 1994, 219), a contract is "a set of promises constituting an agreement between parties, giving each a legal duty to the other and also the right to seek a remedy for the breach of the promises/duties owed to each. The elements of an enforceable contract are competent parties, a proper or legal purpose, consideration (an exchange of promises/duties) and mutuality of agreement and of obligation."

It has been my policy to sit down with my clients and review a blank contract form and potential addenda early in the home-buying process. Then, when it is time to write an actual contract, my clients have a full understanding of the legalities and consequences of the process. This enables them to concentrate on their personal objectives.

Once the buyer makes an offer that is accepted by the seller, the parties are "under contract." A contract concerning the sale of real estate must be in writing, so if any verbal counter-offers were made, and they were not put in writing, they are not enforceable. This agreement sets out the steps to conclude the sale. It identifies the parties and describes the property, the kind of deed, the price, the terms of payment, and many other conditions. Some agreements provide that buyers will lose their deposit if they fail to purchase the property. Many agreements give the seller and the purchaser the right to litigate in court for damages if either party fails to perform.

All contracts should address "what if" situations that may occur and how they will be resolved. For example, will the contract require a buyer to purchase the property even if the buyer is unable to obtain financing? What if there are easements, encumbrances, governmental restrictions or defects that prevent the buyer from using the property in the manner intended? Likewise, the buyers should be protected from litigation and contract obligations if the seller is unable to deliver a proper title or if the condition of the property is other than as described in the agreement. This is true even though a seller may have acted in good faith and was unaware of any title or property defects.

Appraisal

What if the property does not appraise for the negotiated contract price? An appraisal is an estimated value for a property made by a qualified appraiser appointed by the buyer's lender. You can be refused a specific mortgage or offered a lower mortgage amount, if the appraiser's written report is below the established contract sales price. You have various options if faced with this situation. You can make up any difference with a different type of loan, a larger down payment or a renegotiated sales price with the seller. In a quickly appreciating seller's market, such as Northern Virginia, it actually is not unusual for an appraisal to fall short of the price in the sales contract. By federal law, you are entitled to receive a copy of the appraisal, which you and your agent can review and hopefully give the appraiser additional information that will adjust the final appraised value upward.

I'd like to make a few additional points about appraisals. An appraisal is a supported opinion of value. Therefore, the credentials of the appraiser and the accuracy and relevance of the data are critically important. In choosing an appraiser or valuating an appraisal, first examine the credentials of the appraiser.

- How long have they been appraising?

- Do the credentials go beyond the minimums required for basic licensing?

- Do they hold a professional designation such as MAI (Member Appraisal Institute), SRA (Senior Residential Appraiser), IFA (Independent Fee Appraiser) or ASA (American Society of Appraisers)?

When critiquing an appraisal, carefully examine the sales analysis grid. Are the comparable sales including properties which the buyer of the subject property would consider? Are the contract dates, locations and design similar to the subject property?

Remember that for most appraisals, the required Fannie Mae definition of value is "the most probable price which a property should bring in a competitive and open market under all conditions requisite to a fair sale, the buyer and seller, each acting prudently, knowledgeably and assuming the price is not affected by undue stimulus." (The quote is from the Fannie Mae Test Form 1004, November, 2004.) An appraisal is especially useful when you need an unbiased interpretation of the market. An appraisal is frequently required for estate purposes and for many other nonlending purposes.

Finally, many people wonder what the shelf life is of an appraisal. The standard answer in a stable market without rapidly changing values or significant economic changes is about six months. The last time we had such a market in Northern Virginia was in the mid-1990s when there was little fluctuation in prices for a period of time. When inventory is very low or very high, values change more rapidly and an appraised value becomes dated more quickly. An appraisal done at the bottom of the cycle quickly becomes out of date when there is a strong buyer demand and few properties on the market. The opposite is also true.

Contingencies

A good agent can help protect a buyer or seller through the use of contingency clauses in the contract. A contingency is language in the contract that gives one party or the other the right to cancel the contract if certain things about the property are not satisfactory to that party or if the other party fails to meet certain obligations. For instance, a loan contingency clause may require the buyer to apply for a mortgage by a certain date and to get loan approval by another stated date. If the buyer's lender anticipates problems getting loan approval, and cannot provide assurances of loan approval by the required date, then the contract may become void. In that event, the property will be back on the market. As another example, the buyer has the right to review the property homeowner's association documents within a certain time frame. If the buyer finds those documents unacceptable, they can cancel the contract and buy a different property.

There are some less common contingencies that you also may want to consider. For instance, a buyer may request that the purchase of the home be contingent upon the sale of his or her current home. Although this contingency may be rejected—especially in a "hot" real estate market—it still may be sought. You should negotiate for contingencies that you feel are particularly important. You can really ask for any contingency—but do not expect that you will automatically get the other party to agree to it.

Sometimes a contingency can be a key factor for a party deciding whether to finalize the transaction. For example, a seller may be willing to accept a reduced sales price, if they can remain in the home until their new one is built. This enables the seller to avoid an intermediate move, which would require them to store furniture and live in a hotel for a length of time. Thus, a rent back provision is extremely beneficial to the seller! Note, however, that it is important to make all contingency time periods as short as possible in order to expedite the transaction.

Home Inspection

Sellers generally convey property using a "disclaimer document." The Virginia Property Disclosure Act (Statute et seq.) requires that residential property sellers of one to four units disclose, upon the resale of any home, all material information about the property being sold, or allows the seller to provide a disclaimer. Listing agents get this Disclosure/Disclaimer (almost all sellers in Virginia provide a Disclaimer) and present it to the purchaser prior to accepting an offer. The Disclaimer states that the seller makes no warranties as to the condition of the property, which means the onus is on the purchaser to check the property carefully, and at their option, make the contract contingent upon the property being evaluated by a professional home inspector. This being said, it is important to realize that all licensees are required by law to disclose any adverse defects in the property actually known by them. Basically, this means that the seller is "disclaiming" any knowledge of the property's condition. One of the items that a buyer should definitely request in their purchase offer, then, is a contingency for a home inspection performed on the property. This inspection will usually occur one to seven days after the offer is accepted, and it gives the buyer the right to get an accurate technical assessment of a potential future home's condition before being legally committed to buying the property.

There are clauses that permit a property to be sold in "as is" condition. If a property is being sold "as is," the seller may not fix any problems pointed out in an inspection. In a market where buyers are aggressively competing and bidding for properties, sellers often include an "as is" clause. A word of caution, though: you can never be certain about a property's potential problems. I always recommend that my clients include a contingency clause that the sale will depend on the results of a home inspection. However, be aware that a home inspection is not a guarantee of a property's condition.

Regardless of your background, I would never recommend doing an inspection on your own. Typically, inspections only cost one-tenth of 1 percent of the selling price of the home. A good home inspector provides a vital service that gives you security that you have bought a home that will "operate" well after you move in. The inspector should assess the plumbing, the furnace, the electrical system, the drainage of the yard and a host of other issues that most people could not address competently. Unless you are very knowledgeable about structural issues, plumbing and electrical codes, heating and air conditioning, drainage, chimney regulations and roofing practices, inspections are best left to experts. (Even on items that you may feel comfortable with, it is nice to have another set of eyes looking at the house.)

Even if you are buying a newly constructed home, townhouse or condo, I cannot recommend strongly enough that you get a home inspection. The fact that you may pay "megabucks" for a new property does not guarantee that all of the workmanship that went into building that residence is "top-of-the-line."

New home inspections should be conducted periodically throughout the construction process. The inspection conducted during the predrywall phase is most important. At this time the inspector may detect defects that will not be visible after the drywall is installed. Granted, county inspectors will conduct periodic evaluations of a new property as it is being constructed. Due to the rapid pace of new home construction in the Northern Virginia area, though, government inspectors are under serious constraints and cannot spend much time on each inspection. You will want an inspector who will spend hours inspecting your property—not minutes.

Choosing an Inspector

Your agent can be an excellent source of referral for a good home inspector. Many agents work with an inspector on a regular basis who will provide a sound report in which you can have confidence. Home inspectors' competence can vary widely. I recommend that you hire an inspector based on his or her credentials. You will want to find a licensed "Class-A Contractor" with a solid background in inspection, who is also a member or sponsor of ASHI (American Society of Home Inspectors). The ASHI website is *www.ashi.com*. As you are deciding whom to hire as your inspector, you should ask the various candidates some questions:

- How long have you been in business?

- What is your technical background?

- What are your fees?

- Do you have error and omission insurance?

- What certification do you have?

- What is included in the inspection?

- How long will the inspection take?

- What kinds of details will be provided in the inspection report?

You want an experienced inspector who has examined many homes of the type you intend to purchase. If the home has extraordinary traits make sure that the inspector has looked at similar homes in the past.

What an Inspector Should Do

There are certain things that any good inspector will evaluate. Make sure, though, that your inspector is thorough in his review and checks the following items and systems.

- The home's foundation: the inspector should evaluate the crawl space or basement.

- All doors and windows should open and shut properly. If they do not, there may be other structural issues.

- The roof, chimney, gutters, vents and fans should all be in good working order.

- The plumbing should be checked in the kitchen, baths and laundry area. Try to find out how old the plumbing is so that you will know if it will need updating in the near future.

- All electrical systems must be up to code and fully operative.

- The heating and cooling systems should be turned on to ensure that they are operative. This should include examining the ducts, vents, heat exchanger and all safety devices.

- The ceilings, walls and floors should be inspected for structural integrity.

- Insulation should be checked for integrity and depth.

- Ventilation should meet all requirements for the house.

- The quality of the exterior should be looked at—decks, doors, siding, trim, chimney, stucco and sheathing.

- The property should be inspected for any potential indoor environmental concerns, such as radon.

- The basement and attic should be inspected.

- If the inspector suspects lead paint, they should advise you to get the paint tested by an outside expert.

- The inspector should look for FRT (fire retardant) roofing and polybutylene pipes. Pipes made of this material were used for years in new homes in Northern Virginia, and many have broken.

A final note: a general inspector will be knowledgeable about many aspects of a home, but there are some things that an inspector is neither trained nor allowed to do. Your inspector should not tell you what the home is worth, give you advice on whether you should buy the home or offer to make repairs on the home.

Using Other Inspection Specialists

At times, some issues raised by the inspector will need to be addressed by specialists. For certain problems, you should definitely spend the money on a specialist before closing rather than possibly paying the price later. These include structural issues, radon, mold, lead paint and wells or septic tanks.

The potential need for an additional specialist is another reason you will want to be able to trust your original home inspector implicitly. If your home (or the home you intend to purchase) has any of the specific problems listed above, the original inspector will most likely be the one to recommend a specialist and a contractor to resolve the issue.

If circumstances dictate that work must be done to rectify problems in one of these specialty areas, it is especially important that you hire a reputable specialist with a proven track record. I recently had clients who received a contract shortly after listing their home for sale. The contract included the standard "sale contingent on home inspection" clause. The purchaser hired a home inspector who found some mold in trusses in the garage and attic. He recommended a specialist to the buyers to assess the problem. The specialist, in turn, recommended an expensive remedy.

Because of the high estimated cost, we got a second opinion. An experienced home inspector explained to all parties that there are thousands of species of mold; almost all of them are innocuous, and they present no health threat or any other kind of issue other than an aesthetic one. Mold appears in some form in almost every home, on areas ranging from shower curtains to parts of the exterior that are seldom exposed to direct sunlight. He explained further that any mold inspector should take a sample of the mold and send it to an independent laboratory for assessment. Then—after the lab results come back—decide on the proper and most cost-effective action to take, if any were required. To make a long story short, after we insisted on getting the mold tested at a lab, it turned out to be innocuous. My clients avoided a substantial expense that would have been unnecessary.

"Paragraph 3" in Northern Virginia Sales Contracts

The results of your home inspection will address items that are either contractual or noncontractual. Contractual items include those described in Paragraph 3 of the current standard contract used in the Northern Virginia area as of this writing. Regardless of the agreements reached as a result of the home inspection, this paragraph obligates the seller to convey the property and all electrical, heating and cooling systems and appliances in "good working order." Unless the parties involved amend this paragraph, the seller must fulfill this legal/contractual obligation. Paragraph 3 reads as follows:

> **Equipment, Maintenance and Condition**: The Purchaser accepts the Property in the condition as of the Contract date except as otherwise provided herein. The Sellers warrant that the existing appliances, heating, cooling, plumbing, electrical systems and equipment, and smoke and heat detectors (as required), will be in normal working order as of the possession date. The Seller will deliver the Property in substantially the same condition as on the Contract date and broom clean with all trash and debris removed. The Purchaser and the Seller will not hold the Broker liable for any breach of this paragraph.

This language is meant to assure the purchaser that all the equipment and systems in the home will operate when the purchaser takes possession of the house. Obviously, this does not guarantee against any future problems that may arise. Many of the appliances and sys-tems may be operating in good working order—but may also be well beyond their estimated life span. Thus, although their operation fulfills the obligation of the con-tract, buyers must understand that because of the rule of "caveat emptor" (buyer beware), if an appliance breaks down after the new owner takes possession, that new owner must repair or replace it.

Aftermath of the Inspection

At the end of the inspection, the inspector should either review the report with you or take you through the home to point out the items that may need attention. You then have the right to ask the seller to remedy some or all of those items—or you may back out of the con-tract to purchase the house. Be aware that every house has some issues, though. If an inspector does not find any problems, then you may want to question their com-petence! No house is perfect. But don't worry about the "small stuff." For example, if the inspector finds only minimal cosmetic defects—rust stains in the bathroom sink, a deck that needs "power washing," and the like—you may agree to correct these items yourself once you move in.

Still, if there are any major problems, it is completely appropriate for you to request that the seller correct them. If any appliance does not work, the buyer may ask for it to be repaired or replaced per the contract agree-ment. If a deck was not constructed up to code, the buyer may ask the seller to have the deck improved prior to completing the sale or to provide funds in an escrow account to have the repairs done after closing.

The seller can respond to a request for repairs in a vari-ety of ways. They can agree to fix any of these items prior to closing, or refuse on the grounds that the price the buyer negotiated reflected the condition of the residence. Or the seller may offer to settle somewhere in between. For major repairs, the seller may offer compensation at closing and let the repairs be done after ownership has transferred to the buyer. As long as the buyer and the seller can resolve the inspection items to their mutual satisfaction, with everything put in writing, they can proceed to closing.

The Walk-Through

A buyer's "walk-through" is standard in Northern Virginia. At the walk-through, a buyer literally walks through the property just before closing to make sure that repairs agreed to in the contract have been properly finished and that the rest of the property is in substantially the same condition it was at the time of the contract date.

When you do a walk-through, you should try to do it after the sellers have moved out so that you can best assess the condition of the house and make sure that there are no damages from the seller's move. All electrical, heating, and plumbing systems and appliances and mechanical items should be checked to make sure they work as agreed to in the contract. Also, at the final walk-through, a buyer can check to see that all items that are to be conveyed are in place.

By taking these steps in addition to the home inspection, a buyer can be confident that they know everything there is to know about the home. Once the settlement is complete, any problems with the house become the buyer's responsibility. This is why the final walk-through of the property is so important.

Closing

Once you have a firm contract and all contingencies have been removed, your contract is sent, per the agreement in the contract, to an attorney's office or a title company, which is called the settlement agent—a lawyer or a licensed title closer. The settlement agent is a neutral third party representing the contract, not the buyer or the seller. This individual or company will manage all of the necessary paperwork from the seller, the buyer and the buyer's lender as well as arrange for the title examination and title insurance. Only an attorney can prepare legal documents such as the deed of conveyance, which formally transfers the ownership of the property. All reputable title companies have attorneys available to prepare necessary legal documents.

Typically, at real estate closings in Northern Virginia (also referred to as settlements), both parties meet to sign all the necessary documents to finalize the transfer of the property and exchange money and keys. The buyer is responsible for signing most of the documents, as they are largely from the buyer's lender. One of the few documents the seller must sign is the deed of conveyance.

One of the most important documents to be reviewed by all parties at the closing is the settlement statement—typically referred to as the HUD 1 statement—created by the settlement agent. It lists, line by line, each item paid for by the parties involved. There is a buyer's column and a seller's column. The HUD 1 will also show the deposit from the buyer, the loan funding and the proceeds that are to go to the seller. When you sign this statement, you are agreeing that each line item is correct. You must carefully examine and understand the document. Your real estate agent will try to get your HUD 1 ahead of time so you may review it. If you have *any* questions about the HUD 1 figures, be sure to ask questions. Your real estate agent should attend the settlement and be at your side to ensure that the figures and terms are accurate per the contract agreement.

Common Closing Costs	
For the Buyer	**For the Seller**
Settlement and attorney fees.	Settlement fees.
Lender's fees, including document preparation, possible origination fee and underwriting fees.	Attorney fees.
Appraisal fee.	Real estate commission.
Credit report fee (if not paid at the time of loan application). Tax service fees.	Paying off existing loans and any unpaid property taxes, liens, or homeowner fees and obtaining and recording releases for them.
Title insurance premiums.	Termite inspection fees.
Recording fees. One year of homeowner's insurance coverage. Title examination fees. Survey of property. Fee for setting up a tax and home insurance escrow account.	State grantor's tax.

Finally, the settlement agent will record all documents of property ownership. This is done by recording the deed—that is, the legal document conveying title to the property and the deed of trust (in effect, the mortgage) in the county where the property is located. Failure to record certain documents can result in serious legal consequences. The closing agent or title company is responsible for the disbursement of all funds in association with the transaction. This includes sales proceeds, loan payoffs and current taxes. In addition, all liens on the title to the property are to be paid in full and released, ensuring that you take clear title to the property. This is why you want to make sure that a competent, reputable party handles the closing.

Work Performed Prior to the Settlement

To understand the costs involved in the settlement process, you should be aware of the extensive work that has been performed, prior to the actual settlement, by the numerous parties involved. Surveyors, for example, went to measure the property to ensure that the square footage and perimeters of your property registered on the "plat" were accurate. Another individual went to the county courthouse to do a search of the "chain of title" to the property. A professional appraiser, chosen by the mortgage lender, evaluated the market value of the property. A title insurance company examined the title and issued a commitment to ensure title to the property. An attorney drew up legal documents to be signed at the time of closing. A termite inspector went to the property to ensure that there was no burrowing infestation in any wood in the house. A lender put together a "loan package" consisting of various personal financial data, and a lender's underwriter reviewed and approved the package. Individuals from an insurance company may have inspected the property prior to issuing your home fire insurance policy. Representatives from a settlement company determined the required government recording and transfer charges. Fees for all these various services are collected at settlement and properly disbursed.

In other words, when you sit down at a real estate closing for an hour or so and encounter various fees, those charges represent a whole lot of work by many professionals. Their efforts warrant that you are legally protected in the largest purchase of your life.

Further Details on the Settlement Process

Because of the complexity of the settlement process, I would like to offer an expanded discussion of certain aspects of it.

Title Examination

A search of the land records was done on the property to determine that the seller has full legal ownership and the right to convey clear title to the property. You will need to know about any rights or limitations in respect to the property. For example, you must be sure that the current owner (or a previous one) did not sell or give any easements or other rights to portions of the property to another individual or to the local government. The seller probably has used the property as collateral for a loan and placed a lien upon the title. If you are moving into a planned community, the seller may have violated certain covenants or restrictions set forth in the Homeowner's Association rules, including the failure to pay homeowner's dues. These infractions may have resulted in recorded liens on the property you are purchasing. These are matters that a title company would uncover during the title examination. The importance of having a responsible, reputable title company cannot be overstated.

Title Insurance

Title insurance, which is purchased through a one-time fee, is an insurance policy that protects buyers and their lenders against a loss derived from undisclosed or hidden title defects up to the amount insured. If a title problem existed prior to the settlement and was discovered after the settlement, all costs to clear the title are borne by the title insurance company. These costs can include attorney fees and out of court settlements. Your lender will require you to purchase title insurance for the property at closing. This is called a lender's policy. This policy protects *only* the lender's interests from potential title issues. It will cover any losses to the lender up to the existing loan amount. A buyer will also have the option of purchasing "owner's title insurance" at an additional charge. "Owner's title" policies protect the buyer's equity in the property, and in some policies, future equity in the property.

Title insurance affords important protection against financial loss in case of any unanticipated defects to the title. A title insurance company issues title insurance at the time of closing. There are two types of "owner's" title insurance—standard or extended coverage. The extended coverage policies and endorsements are available for an additional premium. You should discuss them with the title company handling your transaction. If you have questions about the difference between the policies or what type of title insurance you need, you may wish to seek the advice of a real-estate attorney.

Why You Need "Owner's Title Insurance"

The lender requires that the purchaser of a property buy the lender's title insurance. I always recommend to my clients that they purchase owner's title insurance as well. When you buy a home, or any property for that matter, you expect to enjoy certain benefits from ownership. For example, you expect to be able to occupy and use the property as you wish, to be free from debts or obligations not created or agreed to by you and to be able to sell or pledge your property freely as security for a loan. Title insurance is designed to ensure these rights for you. This cost can vary, but because it is based on the value of your property, you only pay *once* for title insurance: the coverage continues in effect for as long as you have an interest in the property. If you should die, the coverage automatically continues for the benefit of your heirs. In the event of a claim, there is a provision for payment of all legal expenses for an insured party or that party's heirs.

What Does Title Insurance Cover?

Standard coverage insures against risks such as:

- Forgery and impersonation;

- Lack of competency, capacity or legal authority of a party;

- Deed not joined in by a necessary party (co-owner, heir, spouse, corporate officer or business partner);

- Undisclosed (but recorded) prior mortgage or lien;

- Undisclosed (but recorded) easement or use restriction;

- Erroneous or inadequate legal descriptions;

- Lack of a right of access; and

- Deed not properly recorded.

RGS Title, a prominent settlement company in Northern Virginia, Maryland and Washington, D.C., provided me with the following data on **extended coverage**. In addition to all of the above, some of the additional items you can protect against through extended coverage include defects such as:

- Mechanic's lien coverage provided for work done prior to the date of your policy;

- Zoning coverage, protecting against loss or costs resulting from zoning violations;

- Subdivision coverage in the event that your land is a portion of an improperly created subdivision; and

- Being forced to remove an existing structure, other than a boundary wall or fence, due to a previous owner's failure to obtain the necessary building permit.

Extended coverage also protects you if a neighbor built onto the previous owner's property without permission or if forgeries affected your ownership after the date on which your title insurance policy was issued.

Lender's Documents

Included in the documents that the buyer will have to sign for the lender will be a note and deed of trust—in effect, the mortgage documents. The note creates a formal obligation to repay the lender with whom the buyer has financed the purchase. The deed of trust gives the lender an interest in the property that secures repayment. If the buyer fails to make payments or adhere to the agreements in the terms of the note and deed of trust, that buyer can lose the property through foreclosure.

Deeds

A deed is the instrument that transfers ownership of property from the seller to the buyer. There are several types of deeds, such as general warranty deed, special warranty deed, bargain and sale deed and quitclaim deed. The type of deed affects the buyer's rights against the seller and all former owners. The manner in which the buyer holds title can affect the actual ownership of the property, the owner's tax liability and the owner's estate plan.

There are various ways in which you can hold title to property. Before the deed is filed, you want to determine how you intend to "own" the property. If you are buying a property in conjunction with another person, such as a spouse or relative, you will want to determine what each person's share will be. If you are unsure of the legal consequences of your ownership, you should talk with a lawyer. The following paragraphs, however, generally describe the basic forms of ownership. (Again, RGS Title helpfully provided the data.)

1. Individual or Sole Ownership

This one is simple and straight forward: the property is conveyed to one owner who has the exclusive use and benefit of the property and the right to freely transfer or convey it.

2. Tenancy in Common

Any two or more people (including husband and wife) may hold title this way. If nothing is stated in the deed and there are two or more people on the title, they will hold as tenants in common. Each person has an undivided fractional interest in the property, and the shared right to the use and benefit of the property. That fractional or percentage interest should be expressed in the deed so that it is clear what interest each owner has. In the event of the death of one owner, his or her interest will not pass automatically to the surviving owners; rather, it will vest in the heirs or divisees under his or her will, or pass by the laws of intestacy if no will exists. If there is a recorded judgment against only one of the owners, it will be a lien against the owner's interest, and could subject the entire property to partition and sale in order to pay the judgment. The fractional interest owned by any single tenant may be freely conveyed or transferred to others.

3. Joint Tenants With the Common Law Right of Survivorship

If two or more people (other than husband and wife) hold title, they may choose to be joint tenants with the common law right of survivorship. This right of survivorship must be expressed in the deed, since Virginia has abolished the rights of survivorship otherwise. Should any one owner predecease the other owner(s), title will automatically vest in the surviving owner(s), rather than passing to the deceased owner's heirs or estate. Other than this survivorship provision, the tenancy is essentially the same as tenants in common. Just as with the tenants in common, a lien or judgment against any one owner could be or become a lien against the debtor's interest in the property, and could subject it to a sale in satisfaction of the lien.

4. Tenants by the Entirety

Only husband and wife may hold title in this form of tenancy. The tenancy is based on a legal fiction that the married couple is a single entity and an "entirety" unto itself. It is like joint tenancy in that if one spouse predeceases the other, title to the property will automatically vest in the surviving spouse. The property cannot be conveyed or transferred without both signing the document—one spouse alone cannot transfer any interest. Also a lien or judgment filed against only one spouse will not be a lien against property held with this tenancy. (You should know, however, that the IRS does not acknowledge the "entireties" fiction and may subject the property to its lien against only one spouse.)

Final Thought

You should fully understand any document (especially the agreement to purchase or sell) as well as its terms and consequences. Your agent should explain those to you before you sign any document. As always, whenever there is a contract dispute between a seller and buyer, the best advice I can give is to consult a real estate attorney to decide on the appropriate course of action.

11

Selling Your Home

Selling your home can be an emotional experience. You may have to leave a backyard you enjoy or neighbors with whom you are compatible. The sale can involve the pain of a divorce. Or you can be happily moving on, buying a larger or more attractive home as your family expands or your finances permit. No matter why you are selling your home, you must be ready to take a number of basic steps.

A lot of planning and usually some "financial engineering" go into selling a home. Let's address the financial issues first. On the one hand, you are moving on to your next residence, and it will most likely take discretionary money to make your new home the desirable home you want. You may want to purchase furniture, upgrade the kitchen or enhance the landscaping at your new home. On the other hand, you'd rather spend as little as possible to "spruce up" your existing home to make it attractive to a buyer. You must balance the cost of improving your current home for a rapid sale against the net return you receive as a final sales price. With the extra net profit you may receive from minimal upgrades to your current home, you can budget money for your new home.

You will want to ask yourself the following questions.

- Realistically, how long will my current home be on the market, given the condition of my home, market conditions now and my asking price?

- How urgent is it, for whatever reason, that I sell my home in a short time frame?

- Would my home sell faster and for more profit if I invested money on improvements?

- If I do decide to invest some money to prepare and "stage" my home for a faster sale, how should I invest it?

The answers to these questions will help you determine what you need to do to prepare your home to bring it to the market and sell it quickly.

Is Your Home Ready for Sale?

How do you present your home as attractively as possible to a potential purchaser? The emphasis you place on this depends, again, on many factors—including the condition of your home, the urgency with which you have to sell it, and the price you are asking. If your home is in the "upper brackets," you may want to hire a professional "stager"—an individual who can optimize the appearance of your home at the most reasonable price. Most real estate agents, too, can recommend ways in which to stage your home to make it more saleable. Often, sellers do not maximize the potential sale price simply because they do not properly prepare their home. *The condition that your home is in when the potential buyer sees it for the first time is critical to the successful sale of your home.* **You can't make a second first impression!**

Answers to the questions of how much to spend and which projects will improve the appeal of your home can be complicated, depending on your personal situation. There are some simple, low-cost things you can do to help ensure that the house sells quickly and at the maximum price. You want your home to look its best, even if that just means making it exceptionally clean and organized.

Spring Cleaning

First, clean your house. I am not talking about vacuuming and dusting. I am talking about that type of spring cleaning that your grandmother used to do. Everything should be moved, dusted, mopped, vacuumed and put away. This is a great time to start packing items you will not need in the next few months. Carpeting should be professionally cleaned. Wood should be polished. You want potential buyers to see that the home is sparkling clean—and this costs nothing but some elbow grease.

When you start cleaning, go through your items and get rid of all of the things that you don't plan to take to your next home. Sell them on eBay, donate them to charity or throw them away. Next, start packing things you will not need during the time your home is on the market, even though you will be taking them to your next home.

Some other important "basics":

- Clean out the garage. You may want to store some of your packed boxes neatly in the garage.

- If necessary, rent a small storage unit for the "stuff" that detracts from the appearance of your home but that you plan to move to your new home.

- Clean and organize your closets. Adequate closet space is an important selling feature. If your closets are stuffed full, they will appear smaller.

- Keep the counters in the bathrooms and kitchen as clear as possible. Even if they are outdated, clean counters make the rooms seem larger.

In other words, *minimize* and *organize*. The idea here is to make your home appear as spacious as possible. The less clutter and less furniture that you have, the more open your home will look. If you have furniture that you plan to get rid of, now is the time to donate it to charity or sell it. Buyers like blank slates—and the last thing you want is a dog-worn couch distracting a potential buyer from the beautiful brick fireplace.

Keep the furnishings to a minimum. When a room is cluttered with furniture, the buyer may not appreciate its actual size. Minimizing the amount of furniture is a proven approach to make your home appear the optimal size. As a recent article in *Business Week* noted, "To net top dollar, you have to banish most traces of yourself—from your refrigerator magnets to your kid's artwork—and create an idealized living space, almost with the look of a model home. The goal is to show potential buyers a dwelling that's both tasteful and impersonal enough to allow them to 'mentally move in.' " *You want prospective buyers to say "WOW!" when they enter your home (*Anne Ferguson, "Showtime for Your Home," *Business Week*, Nov. 22, 2004, 172).

Small Projects

From a financial perspective, not all home improvement projects are equal. If you are looking to make improvements to your home before selling, you should make changes in areas that will provide you the highest return on your investment. But even if you can only make a few changes, some small projects can have a real impact.

Without a doubt, a fresh coat of paint can make a world of difference. Although white is bright, it can also look too antiseptic—"hospital-like"—as well as highlight other flaws in a room. At the same time, bright colors can turn some people off. I recommend sticking to warm, mild tones. For a few hundred dollars and a few days work, you can completely warm up the feeling of your home.

Fresh paint also makes a house look cared for and maintained. Painting should include fixing nicks in the wall, scratches from kids or pets and nail pops; caulk, if necessary. Clean, fresh walls tell buyers that your home has been well maintained and is in move-in condition. I promise you that paint speaks volumes. Prioritize this home improvement.

Another important element is flooring. Like the wall paint, the flooring should be neutral, clean and maintained. Nice flooring can make your house more inviting. In some instances, the flooring may need to be changed for the home to get a higher price.

Other Inexpensive Touches

Be sure that your house smells clean and fresh. When potential buyers are coming to view your home—open windows, put out fresh flowers, bake cookies or bread and brew fresh coffee. Avoid air fresheners though, because they usually give the impression that you are trying to cover up bad scents.

Trim and clean up the front landscaping, as this is the first thing that a potential buyer will see. It can cause an immediately pleasing reaction if it looks inviting and maintained. Put away any toys, lawn equipment, trash cans or "junk." *Minimalism is always better than clutter.*

I recommend keeping your cars in the garage or out of the driveway. This gives potential buyers an unobstructed view of your home's exterior features. Paint or stain your front door. Buyers form opinions as agents are ringing the doorbell or opening a lockbox.

Make sure that most lights are on. Your house will appear bright, large and inviting. Years ago, when I worked as an agent at a new-home development, I started my day by opening the model homes and turning on every light.

Larger Projects

Even before the above-mentioned cosmetic changes, you must fix any items that need repair. These repairs should include anything that might cause problems at a home inspection. Bad plumbing, a leaky roof and structural issues, for example, could make selling a house difficult. If your house is in sound condition but could use some updating, experts agree that you will likely get the biggest return on your investment in the kitchen and then in the baths. These rooms seem to go out of style most quickly. Some other items that tend to become outdated (and are worth replacing) are appliances that are more than 10 to 15 years old, linoleum floors, extensive mirrors and dated paneling. Removing wallpaper is a time-consuming and tedious job, but it can depersonalize and neutralize a home for the new buyer.

Valuation and Market Analysis

After preparing your home for sale, the next big step will be determining a fair asking price. An agent will do various forms of research to present you with their opinion of your home's value. The final list price, however, is up to you. Trust your agent's judgment, but make sure that you are comfortable with the asking price. It is your home, and only you can make the final determination on what it is worth to you. If you price it too high, the market will clearly tell you: You simply will not receive a contract or offer on your home. Do not hesitate to reduce the price of your home when the feedback from agents and clients who have looked at the property tells you that the home is overpriced.

There are various ways to determine a realistic price to ask for your home. Here are brief descriptions of some of these methods.

Comparable Market Analysis (CMA)—A CMA shows the prices of comparable homes in your area that have recently sold or are currently on the market. At your request, a Realtor® will do a CMA by analyzing this data. The Realtor® will then determine a price range based on your home's size, condition and the local market. A CMA is not an appraisal.

Appraisal—Some sellers pay $400 to $600 for an estimate of their home's value by a professional, licensed appraiser. Appraisers create a report using homes that have sold and "settled" in the past six months and are comparable to yours. A precontract appraisal estimate can be a useful guideline for setting the sale price of your home. The marketplace is the ultimate determinant, though, and an early appraisal may not take current market conditions into consideration. Also, the purchaser's lender will order a final appraisal for the property. This appraisal is used after a sales contract has been ratified.

Internet pricing—Several websites offer home valuation information for free or for a small fee. These reports don't take into account the condition of the home or important factors such as nearby highways, however. I would not trust a website home evaluation to set a price for your home.

Open houses—Check out open houses in your community. Looking at homes on the market in your area not only lets you check out the competition but also will tell you how your house compares in terms of location, size, amenities and condition. Assuming that all the asking prices were the same, would you buy your home, or someone else's? You may see things that these other homes offer that you can easily and inexpensively add to your home to compete more effectively. Sellers often need an outside, impersonal opinion of value; they have been known to instinctively feel that "my house is much better."

A good agent understands the marketplace and factors current market conditions into his or her recommendation of the right asking price. In a strong seller's market, when homes are increasing rapidly in value, the price suggested by your broker will most likely be higher than what the appraiser can justify in a written report. Many homes have sold for higher than their list prices, and buyers have to adjust their financing accordingly.

If you hire an appraiser to get an estimate for your home before going on the market, it will be for your own peace of mind, but will not necessarily give you the price you should set. In the end, only the marketplace—that is, what a buyer is willing to pay in today's circumstances— will determine the exact price of your home.

Moreover, there will always be buyers who have needs that are not simply reflected by a dollar amount. If you're willing to settle quickly or perhaps extend a settlement date, you may attract buyers who have particular needs in terms of their move. If you can be flexible and meet a buyer's needs, then you will have the best chance of getting a better price in the sale of your home.

The Multiple Listing Service

Nowadays, most people have heard of the Multiple Listing Service (MLS). The MLS has always been the primary way in which agents have found out about houses that are on the market. But today, because the MLS is Internet-based, agents have access to information on a home faster than ever. Also, agents offer their clients access to the MLS through Internet sites, so potential homeowners can view your home with a mouse click just minutes after it is listed.

As you know, consumers who go online primarily want access to current and complete information. Make sure that you work with an agent who will not only quickly post your home on the MLS but will also provide accurate information with as many pictures as possible. With the low cost and ease of digital photography, there is no reason why your home should not get this level of marketing. Effective Internet marketing is not only useful, it is *essential* to the successful sale of your home.

You may have heard that at times "good" listings aren't on the MLS but instead get sold before they come on the market. Although this does sometimes occur, most sellers would rather put a home in the MLS so that it can be seen by numerous real estate agents and untold numbers of potential buyers. Sellers want competition, because it can drive up the price of a home. You want to give as many people as possible access to information about your home.

Interviewing and Choosing a Listing Agent

When I discussed buying a home earlier in this book, I mentioned the possibility of using a buyer's agent to represent you in the transaction. Similarly, when you are selling your home, you should consider working with a seller's agent. A seller's agent is someone who agrees to fulfill certain duties to the seller by entering into an agency relationship with that person. There are many advantages to this relationship. You want to make sure that your interests are protected throughout the transaction, and this can best be achieved by hiring someone to act as your sole representative.

Having a seller's agent will save you almost all the time and trouble involved in selling your house on your own. A good seller's agent will use industry information and market knowledge to help you determine the best listing price for your home. The agent will also market your home to thousands of potential buyers, as well as negotiate the sale all the way through closing. If you don't have time, energy or specialized knowledge about selling real estate, having a trustworthy seller's agent can make selling your home a much smoother transaction.

Beyond helping you determine a fair selling price for your home, seller's agents will make suggestions on how to make your home more appealing so that they can get you the highest possible sales price. They will screen potential buyers and make sure that you only deal with qualified, serious ones. A good seller's agent will market your home to a network of other agents, handle all of the negotiations and paperwork, and oversee the closing process. If you take the time to find and hire an experienced, well-qualified, full-time real estate agent, it will make a world of difference.

What to Look for in a Listing Agent

You want an experienced agent who knows how to get a home sold. A good listing agent will have the following qualities as well.

- An agent needs to be trusted and respected in the community for their integrity in the real estate business.

- An experienced agent has a track record of many successful sales transactions and has a large referral and repeat business clientele.

- Many good agents have a business support staff. This can take the form of a team member, an assistant, a real estate partner or even a virtual assistant.

- An agent should have an Internet presence, an email address and proficiency in today's technology. The ability to have virtual tours and digital photos of your home on the Internet is a benefit. Over 80 percent of all buyers begin their home-buying process by using the Internet. Talk about an unlimited number of potential buyers!

- A good agent will invest in their business through websites, work in the community, mailings, promotions, advertising, custom stationery, presentation packages and so forth.

- An agent who has multiple advanced professional designations shows their commitment to the profession.

Remember to ask a potential listing agent for references—and ask other questions, too. What types of marketing does the agent use? How does the agent use technology to sell homes? Does the agent have a website and network with other agents? How many homes did the agent sell in the last year?

Make sure you do your homework and find an excellent agent who will work hard to sell your home. If you choose to work with a seller's agent, you will be required to sign a listing agreement. This agreement obligates you to work only with that agent to sell your home during a designated period of time. My team has an "easy exit program" from any listing agreement. This means that if for any reason the seller is not totally satisfied with the team's service, the seller can exit the listing. I'm proud to say that none of my clients have ever invoked this option. Check with your prospective agent to see if an easy exit clause is part of the agreement.

Accountability

Under Virginia law, seller's agents—like buyer's agents—have certain obligations to their clients. A seller's agent owes the home seller the following affirmative duties:

- to exercise reasonable care and diligence;

- to deal honestly and in good faith;

- to present all offers, notices and other communications to and from the parties in a timely manner without regard to whether the property is subject to a contract for sale or the buyer is already a party to a contract to purchase;

- to disclose material facts known by the seller's agent that are not apparent or readily ascertainable to a party;

- to account in a timely manner for money and property received from or on behalf of the seller;

- to be loyal to the seller by not taking action that is adverse or detrimental to the seller's interest in a transaction;

- to disclose in a timely manner to the seller any conflict of interest, existing or contemplated;

- to advise the seller to seek expert advice on matters related to the transaction that are beyond the agent's expertise;

- to maintain confidential information from or about the seller except under subpoena or court order, even after termination of the agency relationship; and

- unless agreed otherwise in writing, to make a continuous, good faith effort to find a buyer for the property, except that a seller's agent is not required to seek additional offers to purchase the property while the property is subject to a contract for sale.

For Sale By Owner (FSBO)

People decide to sell their homes for many reasons. They may be relocating for work; the house may be too small for their current needs; they may be retiring; they may be buying a "dream home." For some people, moving is more attractive than trying to remodel their current home to make it "fit." Whatever the reason for selling *your* home, it is an enormously important financial transaction. In order to make wise decisions, you should make sure that you are both educated and well prepared.

With the potential savings you might accrue by not having to pay a commission to a real estate agent, you may be considering selling your house on your own. Due to the potential legal liability and very complicated technical aspects of this transaction, though, it is not easy to do. It certainly can be done—some people do it successfully every year. But whether they go it alone or work with an agent, the most successful home sellers take an active role in the process.

If you are not absolutely prepared and knowledgeable when selling your own home, you may be in for some trouble. A knowledgeable agent can actually get you thousands of dollars more and save you the headaches involved in both finding a buyer and negotiating a contract and sale. "For Sale By Owner" (FSBO) contracts have a much higher chance of not closing or settling when compared to contracts in which an agent is involved.

Let me make an extremely important point. *There is a legal liability involved in selling a home.* If you decide to sell your home on your own and you even *unintentionally* mislead a buyer, you may be hearing from a lawyer. A good agent can help you make a sound financial decision *and* protect you from possible liability. I want to be as impartial as possible, so I am going to start by giving you information on going it alone, but I also want you to be aware of the complications that can arise when you are attempting to sell your home without a professional agent.

Selling On Your Own

Start by familiarizing yourself with each element involved in selling a home. First, you must decide on how to price your home. You may need to pay for an appraisal. Regardless of how you determine the price, proper pricing is essential.

The longer your house sits on the market, the harder it will be to sell. Homes that are sold by their owners normally sit on the market longer than homes sold by professionals. They are usually underexposed to the market and not properly priced. Indeed, buyers commonly assume that homes sold by owners on their own are overpriced. Buyers also expect to get some type of compensation for the money you are not paying in commissions. Of course, this compensation may take the form of an offer that is well below the asking price. If the buyers choose to also go into the process without representation, they will want to be compensated (again, through a lower price for your home) for the effort that they will have to put into the transaction.

When selling your home on your own, you must be prepared to market your home to as many potential buyers as possible. You will want to have a sign in your yard, an ad in the newspaper and an Internet listing. You will then need to have open houses—which also must be advertised in the paper—and provide fact sheets for potential buyers. (Buyers would get these from an agent if the house were being sold by a professional.)

Once you are ready to negotiate, you want to make sure that you only work with preapproved buyers—that is, buyers who have been approved by a lender to purchase a home that is equal to your asking price. If not, the financing issue could very well kill the transaction. You would have to start the process over. You may also want to be willing to work with a buyer's agent (an agent representing the buyer). Although you will have to pay the agent a commission, that person will ultimately help with the details to make sure that the sale goes through for the client.

If there are no professionals involved, you need to know how to deal with all of the paperwork. Selling a home involves multiple legal contracts. Forms are available, but you must make sure that you are using the right forms and that they are filled in properly to protect your rights. I encourage you to hire an attorney to oversee your actions, or you may be tied up in the legal system as you attempt to resolve problems.

You will also need to find an attorney or title company to handle the settlement. This is relatively simple, but you will want to enlist one early on in the process so you don't find yourself improperly handling a buyer's deposit or escrow funds.

Pros of Selling Your Home on Your Own

- There is no brokerage fee (commission) to be paid. You receive all of the proceeds, less marketing costs.

- You are in total control of the transaction.

- If mistakes are made, they are your own.

- You will be the one available at the home for show-ings and will answer inquiries. This way, you will know how your home is being described to others.

Cons of Selling Your Home on Your Own

- Many buyers believe that if you sell on your own and don't pay a commission, they, not you, should get the savings. This is because the buyer must keep tabs on the mortgage lender, the appraiser and the home inspectors to make sure that everything is ready at closing.

- You bear all marketing and advertising costs, which can be expensive.

- You must be able to analyze the quality of an ap-proval letter of the buyer.

- Without the proper background and knowledge, you may underprice or overprice your home.

- You may lose money during the negotiating pro-cess, lose out on a qualified buyer or sell your home at too low a price if you are not skilled in negotia-tion.

- You are responsible for handling all of the paper-work and legal forms, such as the many required disclosures and contingencies the buyer may come up with.

- You will need to spend a great deal of time showing your property to people you do not know.

- The seller must keep in touch with the buyer to make sure that everything is completed, such as get-ting the mortgage, homeowner's insurance and ap-praisal.

- You must educate yourself about legal and financial issues to be most effective.

You "Sold" Your Home—Now for the Hard Part

Let's say you've decided to go the FSBO route; then, just a few weeks after being on the market, you get a contract at a price you are willing to accept. You tell everyone at work—and your neighbors—"I sold it."

Not so fast. Have you asked yourself how qualified the potential purchaser was in terms of his or her ability to obtain a mortgage? If the purchaser already owns a home, and the contract is subject to the sale of that home, how motivated is the buyer to sell their current home? How realistically is that home priced? How marketable is it? How much time can you take off from work to carry out the functions of a agent?

Innumerable details must be worked out before the proposed transaction actually comes to fruition. A good agent would, for instance, do the following *after* a contract is signed:

- negotiate and follow through with the resolution of all contract contingencies;

- evaluate the quality of your purchaser's preapproval letter;

- communicate with your purchaser's loan officer;

- track the process of your purchaser's home sale;

- order all of the homeowner and/or condo documents needed for the settlement and ensure that any violations get resolved before then;

- meet with the appraiser at your property and present him or her with pertinent information, such as comparable home sales in the neighborhood and the upgrades that have been made to your property;

- evaluate the appropriate paperwork to make certain the title insurance, deed, land survey and (if necessary) power of attorney documents are ready for the settlement;

- review all inspection reports with you;

- negotiate all addenda to the contract and resolve any problems that may arise in the postcontract/presettlement time frame;

- maintain communications with any other agent involved in the transaction, and attend the settlement to help ensure that all the paperwork and the final figures are accurate and that everything goes smoothly.

Selling a home on your own may save you money in certain cases, but many problems and challenges can arise—including holding open houses, attracting potential homebuyers, selling within a planned length of time and dealing with the increasing complexity of the transaction. The process has more disclosures and legal requirements than ever before. Even if you are lucky enough to find a potential buyer quickly, a significant percentage of FSBO transactions break down before getting to the settlement. Again, you must be prepared for every part of the negotiations.

About five years ago, an individual I knew put up his home "For Sale By Owner." He soon received a contract from someone who wanted to buy it, but the purchaser had to sell her home. The buyer included in the contract a provision that the purchase of the home was contingent on the sale of the buyer's current home. A few days later, the seller received a full-price, no-contingency contract from another buyer, and the seller accepted that contract. He called the first purchaser and informed her that he was sorry, but he had sold the home to someone else. She replied, "You'll be hearing from my lawyer."

The seller had not realized that the first purchaser had the "right of first refusal." In other words, if another buyer came along, the first buyer had the right to drop her contingency and buy the home. (Furthermore, because the owner of the home had not done the proper research, he put his home on the market at a price below what it could have received. Both buyers, then, were very motivated to succeed in their purchase of the home.) The second purchaser then hired a lawyer, as did the homeowner. The case dragged on for almost two years.

12

Protecting Your Investment and Upgrading Your Home

Obviously, when you own a home, you should protect your investment. You can buy a home warranty policy, which will cover your expenses if something goes wrong after you move into your home. In some cases, the policy will cover the cost of replacing appliances or parts of systems. With the proper maintenance of your home, fewer items will need repairs or replacement over the years. And, of course, you will want to insure your home to protect you and your family from the unforeseen. Here are the major ways of protecting the investment you have made in your property.

Home Insurance

Earlier in the book, I covered the topic of "credit scores" and their impact on one's qualifying for a mortgage. I briefly described the major factors that go into determining one's credit score and how, if necessary, it can be improved. I also listed the web addresses of the websites of the three primary credit bureaus. Many readers may not be aware, however, that there is also a massive data base—kept current by corporations that insure homes and automobiles—which gives you as an individual and the property you own (or the property you intend to purchase) an *"insurance score"*. This insurance database is referred to as CLUE (Comprehensive Loss Underwriting Exchange).

Stated simply, CLUE is a clearinghouse of information. The CLUE database is not maintained by an insurance company, but about 600 insurance companies contribute information to the database. The history of any insurance claim will show up in this database. *The price you will pay for your home insurance policy is affected by this CLUE report.* In fact, the property might be "blacklisted" by insurers. You should get a copy of your home's CLUE report and also one on any home you intend to purchase. You can get a CLUE report online or through the mail. Extensive information on this topic is contained at the following website: *www.choicetrust.com/pdfs/curious_consumer_form.pdf.* Another insurance database is maintained by the Insurance Services Office (ISO). Their reports on properties are referred to as an A-PLUS Report. Their website is: *www.iso.com/offices_contacts/index.html.*

If you have a mortgage, the lending institution will require you to have homeowner's insurance to cover the replacement value of the home. This ensures that the bank's asset is protected—because in reality you don't own your home until your mortgage is paid off. Basic homeowner's insurance covers items such as loss from fire, loss from natural causes (excluding earthquakes and floods) and the theft of personal belongings in your home. The insurance can cover you if someone falls or gets hurt in your home and you are sued.

You should also consider other types of insurance, depending on where you are located. They can protect you from the financially and emotionally devastating effects of losing a home. Most important, you should make sure you get personal property coverage, which covers your personal possessions. You should keep an inventory of your possessions in the event that a loss occurs. Take digital pictures—or put a walk-through of your house on the video camera—and then store the data at your office or at a relative's home. If a loss does occur, these invaluable records will help provide proof to the insurance company of what was lost so that you can replace these items if necessary.

Basic insurance policies generally protect you against the following events. (These may or may not be covered by your particular policy, so be sure to discuss the details with your insurance agent before choosing any type of coverage.)

- Fire

- Wind

- Accidental explosion

- Smoke damage

- Broken glass

- Theft

- Vandalism

- Personal injury

You may also opt to purchase insurance against burst pipes, falling trees, earthquake, flood and erosion.

Home Warranties

A home warranty is a homeowner's best defense against costly repairs or complete replacement of existing systems and appliances that could break down from normal wear and tear. Whether your home is new or old, a home warranty can provide you with the security of knowing that your systems and appliances are protected for a predetermined period of time. Home warranty plans are generally not very expensive. They usually cost about $400 to $500 a year and can be renewed for as long as you own the home. Home warranties must be purchased within 21 days of closing, and they will cover all of the items that are in good operating condition at the time the plan is purchased. Your agent will have information on multiple home-warranty companies and should be able to help you decide if a home warranty is right for you. Home warranties generally cover plumbing (including the water heater); electrical systems; appliances, including dishwasher, refrigerator, stove and washer and dryer; heating and air conditioning; garage door openers; and pest control. For an extra charge, you can usually add wells, pools, roofs and windows.

Upkeep of Your Home

Just as you regularly change the oil in your car to ensure that it lasts and operates well, you can extend the life of the "systems" in your home with normal maintenance. Regular care will save you not only money but also the trouble associated with surprise home repairs. Use the following checklist to keep track of important home systems.

- Conventional filters on forced-air systems should be checked monthly and cleaned or replaced as needed. Electronic filters, too, should be checked monthly and cleaned as needed. Make sure the interior components are installed in the correct orientation after cleaning. Noises should be brought to the attention of a technician. Furnaces and boilers should be inspected every year to make certain that all the components are operating properly and no connections are loose or burned.

- Electric furnaces should be inspected every year to ensure that all the components are operating properly and that no connections are loose or burned. Electric baseboard heaters should be kept clean.

- Have your ducts cleaned at least every five to six years. This keeps your furnace clean and will increase its life expectancy. Make sure your ducts have no cracks or leaks in the ductwork, and apply special tape to any cracks or openings.

- Drain the water heater tank at least every year and flush it out. To remove any buildup on the elements, soak in vinegar, then scrape off any scales.

- Do not plug more than a few appliances into one circuit.

- When using the air conditioner, check the filters once a month.

- Once a year, clean the coils on the back or underneath the refrigerator.

- Clean the garbage disposal regularly by pushing a full tray of ice cubes through it while running cold water. Always remember to run water during use, and for at least two minutes after you finish, to prevent stoppages.

- Clean the lint screen in the dryer after each load of clothes is dried and the unit is empty.

- Regularly check for cracks in the walls and the foundation. Cracks and voids should be filled. (Filling cracks allows for easy monitoring of movement between inspections.)

- Have the roof checked periodically for cracked or missing tiles or shingles, and replace these immediately.

- Gutters are an important part of your home's weatherproofing. You will need to maintain a free-flowing gutter system, as your gutters prevent rain from running off your roof and falling too close to your house. Diverting water from your house properly will protect your foundation, keep stains from developing on your siding and keep walkways ice-free in the wintertime. Clean your gutters monthly if there are tall trees near your house.

Upgrading Your Home

Beyond following a sound maintenance program to protect the value of your property, you should consider the impact of upgrades on the value of your home. The options for upgrading your home are almost unlimited. Though baseball is known as "the great American pastime" home improvements must be a very close second. Americans spent over $250 billion in 2004 upgrading their homes. I'm sure that you have read articles in a number of magazines about which types of upgrade projects will give you the best return on your investment when you eventually sell your home. I'm not an expert in this area, but I offer my perspective as an agent and homeowner.

As you make a decision on how much you should spend on upgrade projects and which projects you should proceed with, I recommend that you think about your lifestyle, the cost of upgrades and how long you plan to live in the home.

Approaching Upgrades

I have recently been in the process of upgrading my home. The first decision I made was to have a professional come in to offer advice and make recommendations. Ironically, we sometimes fail to see the shortcomings of the very home in which we live! When the decorator walked in, the first thing she said was, "This home is too dark." Sure enough, the drapes and the paneling in the family room did not give my home a bright feeling or cheery atmosphere. I decided to make changes.

Based on her advice, I started with the kitchen. Kitchens are always near the top of the list in terms of the return on your upgrading investment. Now, if you get really serious about upgrading a kitchen, you can spend extraordinary amounts of money. Have you priced cherry wood cabinets? (I'm not talking about pricing them by going to a top-of-the-line custom kitchen contractor. Just go to Home Depot or Lowe's to see what cherry wood cabinets cost.) Similarly, granite cabinet tops and appliances such as Viking stoves or sub-zero refrigerators are very expensive. You should consider your lifestyle as you approach upgrading decisions. Take my case, for instance: My husband and I are empty-nesters, we don't entertain often, and my cooking abilities can euphemistically be described as "limited." (In fact, I have memorized the phone numbers for about eight restaurants in the area near our home.) Thus, we chose to approach the kitchen upgrades in a low-cost mode: refurbish the cabinets, purchase moderately priced appliances and so on. Obviously, many folks are at the opposite extreme—gourmet cooks, frequent entertainers, parents with children at home—and would rightly prefer going all-out with their kitchen upgrades. My point is that you should think about what is really important to you and your family. The money you save by going "low dollar" on one aspect of upgrading frees up funds to do other things which may be of higher priority.

Given the key role that computers and the Internet play in so many of our lives, having a study or home office that is well wired, well furnished and comfortable, may be a very high priority for you and your family. Adding or improving a deck, patio or screened-in porch can be done at a relatively modest cost and will be a "slam dunk" in terms of improving the appeal and value of your property.

Some folks get excited about the interior of the garage. To many, a garage is just a place to park the car, put the garbage and store stuff. To others it's a place for nifty tools and lawn implements, and it provides them a "space" to work on projects. Have you ever seen the ad that appears in some magazines for a complete system of storage bins, tool storage boards and lockers to keep a garage organized? It's called the Gladiator System! On a serious note, it can be nice to have one—it improves the appearance of the garage and adds to the overall appeal of your home.

Of course, the number of years you intend to live in the home should have a significant impact on your upgrade decision. Obviously, if you are in a starter home and intend to "move on up" within a few years, socking money away to upgrade your next home would be wiser than spending a lot of money on your current residence. Obviously, this is especially true for any potential investment in "big ticket" items or upgrades.

Landscaping

Landscaping is in a special category: it is undoubtedly one of the most cost-effective ways to increase the value of your property. Even if you are planning on staying in a home for only a few years, putting some money and "sweat equity" into landscaping is wise. Not only will your property be more attractive and enjoyable while you live there, it will also be more appealing to potential purchasers when you decide to sell.

When I work with clients who are in the process of buying a home, I put together a list of homes that are in their price range and reflect the style of home they desire. I can't tell you the number of times I have pulled up in front of a home that fits the general description and heard the client say, "We don't have to bother to go in to see this one." They have bad "vibes" based on their initial impression! "Curb appeal" is crucial. Obviously, landscaping is a very important component of curb appeal. If you are in a home for the long haul, you should consider hiring a professional landscape architect for your landscaping upgrade.

13

Investing in Real Estate in Addition to Your Primary Residence

Owning real estate is valuable for the roof it puts over your head, the enjoyment you get from living in your home, the increased net worth you gain from home ownership and the extensive tax breaks you get during that ownership. *Directly investing in real estate other than your primary home can make a key additional contribution toward achieving your long-range financial goals.* Making smart real estate purchases and buying investment properties can increase your net worth significantly.

The experience you have gained from buying and living in your home gives you an excellent background for taking the next step of buying additional properties, should you decide to do so. I strongly recommend that you consider having a lifelong real estate investment plan—beyond owning your primary residence—as a way to diversify your assets and maximize your long-term wealth and that of your heirs.

Investment Options

Most types of investments are broken down into three general categories: *fixed income investments, equities* and *direct ownership of real estate.* Fixed-income investments include certificates of deposit (CDs), money market funds, notes and bonds. These investment options provide you with a safe place for your savings. Equities include the direct ownership of individual stocks, owning a "group" of stocks through mutual funds, owning REITS (Real Estate Investment Trusts), buying stock put and call options or buying "preferred" stocks. Also, you can own real estate—residential or commercial property—directly. Let's take a few moments to compare these alternatives.

Certificates of Deposit, money market funds, notes and short-term to intermediate-term bonds—all fixed-income investments—offer the safest opportunities for investing, but they also provide you with a low return on your investment. Most folks will never become rich if they rely exclusively on these forms of investing. Nevertheless, these types of investments should play a role in your long-range financial goals.

The second avenue—equities—has been an enormously successful investment for many. Overall (and over the very long term), the stock market has returned annual gains that are superior to any other form of investing. Note, though, that the long-term trend has included enormous stretches of time when the stock market return was basically flat. For example, from 1964 to 1982, the

Dow Jones Industrial Average traded in such a narrow range that there was no capital gains at all if you owned and held on to each stock in the DJIA during that 17-year period. Conversely, there was an enormous increase in the value of equities between 1982 and 2000, but many of those gains—especially in the more speculative "Over the Counter" market—quickly evaporated in the implosion of many technology stocks. So if you are an investor who is convinced that you can beat "Mr. Market" over the long term, be careful. The bottom line, at least from my perspective, is that many folks may rely too heavily on their stock portfolio (or their 401k plan invested in stocks) and may not achieve the fine life in their retirement that they so richly deserve.

Direct investment in real estate in addition to your primary residence covers various investment options, including residential and commercial real estate as well as land itself. You should be fully aware up front that a direct investment in real estate (other than land) requires a lot of attention and needs active management. Remember, when you invest in real estate, you are investing in your future. You should anticipate your future needs and those of your family when buying and selling property. You want to make your investment work for *you*!

Your initial direct investment in real estate will have the potential to skyrocket, thus giving you solid gains for your retirement without having to worry about the risks of stock ownership for that portion of your diversified assets. No other investment provides the security and cash flow that real estate does. If you are in it for the long haul, regardless of market swings, investments in property almost always pay off. The benefits of home-ownership, discussed in Chapter 2, obviously also hold true for investing in investment properties—especially the leverage and the tax advantages that will bring you a great return on your investment over the years. In fact, there are additional tax breaks related to investment properties (including depreciation). Granted, directly investing in real estate is different from other forms of investing, because it requires more attention and needs active management. But in my estimation the benefits far outweigh the time and effort required.

There are three major advantages to buying rental property.

- A real estate investment can provide a great deal of leverage. Today, you can purchase a rental property in many locations in the United States for as little as 10 percent down, thus obtaining a 90 percent mortgage loan.

- The tax code provides significant tax benefits for your annual return—including depreciation, deducting interest on the mortgage payments and writing off operating expenses and any investments you make in improving your investment property.

- The tax code also provides significant benefits for the long term when you decide to sell one investment property and invest in another. IRS Section 1031—commonly referred to as the "Starker Exchange"—allows you to defer long-term capital gains tax even if you buy and sell numerous investment properties over the years. A 1031 exchange allows owners of certain types of income property to sell their property and buy similar property without paying any capital gains tax. The "similar kind of property provision" of Section 1031 is quite broad, and it includes land, rental properties and some commercial properties. Any of these can be exchanged for another version of the same type of property without being taxed. The rule requires the owner of the property to use a "qualified intermediary" as a safe harbor to hold the proceeds while the exchange is in progress. A qualified intermediary is a professional licensed to hold funds for transfers of real property. There are also strict time limits. For example, you must identify a new property within 45 days after the close of the primary property, and the closings must occur within 180 days of each other. It should be noted that Section 1031 does not apply to "related party" transactions. The many other rules and restrictions can be outlined for you by either an accountant or a qualified intermediary. The bottom line is that a 1031 exchange allows investment property owners to benefit from buying more expensive income properties without being taxed on the appreciation of the properties they've sold.

Envisioning Your Investment Property

If you decide to invest directly in real estate beyond your primary residence, I suggest that you break any potential purchases into three categories. First, you may want to buy a second home—a vacation residence. Second, you may choose to purchase land or an investment property in an area where you might want to retire. It would be best to make such an investment well before your actual retirement. The third approach is to buy a condo, townhouse or detached home or apartment building (or multiple sites) as an investment with the goal of increasing your total net worth and providing an additional source of income. Let's briefly overview.

Vacation Properties

Buying a vacation home may indeed fit into a well-thought-out financial strategy. One of my sons recently went to a financial planner who analyzed his family's overall financial situation. The objective of the exercise was to develop a wide-ranging plan that took all aspects of the family's financial situation into consideration, ranging from getting proper insurance coverage to setting up 529E college savings plans for the children and making rough estimates on the eventual value of his 401k and corporate retirement plans. I found it interesting when my son mentioned to me that the financial advisor's final report suggested that the purchase of a vacation home should be given strong consideration as a component of an overall long-range financial plan.

Obviously, investing in a vacation property is very personal. Individuals, couples and families have widely ranging interests and desires for their recreation properties that could include ski lodges, golf resorts, lakeside or oceanside properties, hunting areas or a condo in a metropolitan area. If you vacation often, paying exorbitant rental prices or hotel fees season after season can be very expensive. Investing in a vacation property can end up saving you money while giving you a comfortable place in which to spend your vacations.

The purchase of a vacation home can also pay off profitably in terms of the money you will make from renting your home out to other vacationers when you are not there. If you purchase a vacation home in a desirable resort area, you can rest assured that people will always compete for rentals, especially during peak seasons and long weekends. There may be additional mortgage interest deductions for your second home, too. (These deductions should first be verified by your accountant.) The value of your vacation property may also increase significantly over the years if you select it wisely.

Retirement Properties

You might consider buying a lot or land in a community where you plan on retiring at some future date. If that interests you, I would like to mention an option that may be attractive to some. The editor of *Forbes*, Richard Kaargland, recently wrote a book that hypothesized that the "next big thing" in residential real estate might be the rapid growth of home values in "university towns." He notes that home prices are so high in the cities where many of the largest corporations are headquartered that those corporations are encountering trouble when they ask employees to move to those locations. After all, many people would find it difficult to give up a nice four-bedroom colonial on an acre lot in a city in the Midwest to make a lateral move (at least in terms of home value) to a greatly downsized residence in some major metropolitan areas.

On the other hand, university towns or cities—such as Madison, Wisconsin; Ann Arbor, Michigan; Charlottesville, Virginia; and Chapel Hill, North Carolina—offer a lively social setting and an appealing, "youthful" environment. The real estate costs in many of these areas are modest. Kaargland projects that corporations may begin to relocate to these moderate sized but dynamic cities where universities are located. He anticipates that these locations may very well see a rapid increase in real estate values.

Various magazines have featured articles about people who decide to retire (or semi-retire) in the town or city where they attended college. They have the advantage of already being familiar with the community and probably have made at least occasional contacts with these cities by returning for class reunions or homecoming football games. If returning to your college town for your "golden years" appeals to you, you might consider buying a properly zoned lot or a rental property in that town, or its environs, well before your actual retirement begins.

Many people hope to retire to more typical locations—North Carolina, Florida or Arizona, for example. If that happens to be your plan, I would still recommend looking into investing in those locations well before your actual retirement—whether it be in a lot, a townhouse or a detached home that you may eventually want to live in.

A Theoretical Retirement Case

Let's address a hypothetical case. You are 50 years old, and your long-range goal is to retire at age 65 with a very comfortable lifestyle. You have a modest 401k plan and you've been contributing to Social Security over the years. At age 50, you decide to diversify your assets to help achieve your long-range financial goals, and you purchase a rental property—let us say a townhouse. You take out a 15-year mortgage on that investment property. During the first five years of this investment, you have a slightly negative cash flow, even after the tax breaks you get from depreciation and deducting the interest payments on your mortgage payment. During the next five years of your 15-year mortgage, you basically break even. In the last five years of the 15-year mortgage, you see a modest monthly profit, but you reinvest a portion of that profit into the property because you make upgrades. At first glance, this does not appear to be a very good deal; in terms of cash flow, you've basically had a modest profit over the 15 years. What's the big deal? Why go down that investment road? Here is why!

The Payoff!

If the value of property has increased by just an average value of 5 percent at a compounded rate over that 15-year period, the total value of your property is up 100 percent. (Note: This is a very modest assumption in Northern Virginia. In Fairfax County the gains have been in double digits for each of the last five years.) Your "out of pocket" money for this investment over the 15-year period has been basically just the down payment. Let's go on.

At the end of the 15 years (again, based on rental income examples from townhouses in Northern Virginia), your monthly income from that property in today's dollars (2005) would be in the range of $1,500 to $1,700. You have no payment (other than taxes and upkeep) to make on the property, because your mortgage is paid off.

If you time your mortgages so that both your rental property and your personal residence are paid off simultaneously (and for discussion purposes, let us also assume a payment of $1,500 per month for your personal residence), your monthly cash flow has suddenly changed dramatically. You no longer have monthly mortgage payments of $3,000 for the two mortgages, and you have a monthly income of $1,500 from the rental property. Let's take that one step further. Your sixty-fifth birthday also works out to be the time that you begin to receive $1,700 per month from Social Security. Suddenly, based on this scenario, your positive net annual cash flow has shifted dramatically in your favor. These estimates do not include any income you may derive from corporate retirement plans, government retirement plans or IRAs and 401ks.

Many folks get involved in investing in real estate as a way to accumulate assets. They may buy properties that are in default, purchase "fixer-uppers" and then repair them or "flip" properties—i.e., put an "earnest deposit" down on a property that has not been built and then sell it as soon as it's complete. There are innumerable books to read or seminars to attend if you choose such aggressive investment paths. In this chapter, I'm simply recommending that you consider broadening your investment horizon to include direct investment in real estate. Over the long term, you may accrue enormous wealth and income from such an investment.

Naturally, as discussed throughout this book, I believe that buying real estate should start with the selection of a qualified agent. The same holds true for buying investment properties. You need to make sure that your agent is willing to commit to an exclusive buyer agency agreement with you. Purchasing rental property is actually far easier and less stressful than purchasing your own home. Once you set up your investment objectives and property parameters and get the commitment of your agent, you merely have to wait until a property meeting your investment criteria becomes available. Because you are never going to live in the property, the floor plan needs only to be average for the area.

Landlord-Tenant Basics

Rental properties can be an excellent investment in any market. As noted, few investment alternatives can provide you with significant appreciation, a nice monthly cash flow and generous tax breaks. But unlike other investments, you can spend a substantial amount of time and energy managing your investment (i.e., being a landlord). If you are considering buying real estate as an investment, here are some landlord-tenant basics that you should know.

Under Virginia law, any dwelling place that you rent out to another person must be habitable. Check with your agent on the details of what must be provided. If you are considering buying a "fixer-upper" rental property that needs a new roof, windows or other essential item, be sure that you have the funds to fix them immediately or that you ask the seller to fix them in your sales contract. It is simply illegal to rent a place, even for a short period of time, without repairing such items. This chapter is just touching on the basics of owning rental property, so if you intend to buy rental property, do your homework on Virginia's landlord-tenant laws.

Information Every Landlord Should Know

The number one basic rule—which is from the Virginia Fair Housing Act—is that you must never discriminate against anyone on the basis of race, color, religion, national origin, sex, elderliness, familial status or handicap. You also may not refuse to rent to adults with young children. There are exceptions to this rule, with "adult only" communities and buildings. Discrimination is a serious matter in housing and is not taken lightly by the state.

Make sure that you have a written lease with your tenants. The lease can be for a month-to-month period, in which any party can end the tenancy at any time with 30 days' notice, or it can be for a set period of time, such as six months or two years. You have the right to charge prospective tenants a reasonable application fee. After a tenant moves out you have 45 days to refund the tenant's entire deposit or to explain to the tenant, in writing, why some of the deposit is being held back. Make sure you are familiar with the items that are allowed to be withheld from a deposit.

If you sell or buy a building with tenants, you are obligated to honor the terms of the original rental agreement. You will also be responsible for returning any deposits when the tenants move, so make sure that you get the deposit money from the old landlord. Although there is no rent control in Virginia, you can only raise the rent at the end of the lease term (or within 30 days, if the tenant has a month-to-month lease). You may charge a late fee if the rent is not received by a stated date in the lease.

You have the right to enter a tenant's unit, but you must give a verbal or written reasonable notice before entering, unless there is an emergency or a prior agreement to let you enter.

If you have grounds to evict a tenant, you must use the judicial system to get the tenant out of the unit. You can be held legally responsible if you change the locks, shut off the utilities, remove the tenant's belongings or take any other action outside the courthouse to force the tenant to move. Some lawful reasons for evicting a tenant are as follows: refusing to move after the expiration of a lawful 30-day notice; unlawfully keeping a pet in violation of the lease; being more than seven days late in paying rent; unlawfully renting or subletting the unit or letting others reside in it (not counting temporary guests); and injuring or threatening injury to anyone in the building or any other extreme and outrageous behavior. (You may want to consult with an attorney.)

Good Tenants

As someone who has been a landlord over the years, I want to share an important lesson that I have learned: hold on to good tenants! In some of my rental properties, I have not raised the rent for an extended period of time. The tenants were pleased with the property and the rent that was charged. I received a good return on my investment and minimized the costs of finding new tenants. All parties were satisfied.

APPENDIX A

Glossary
of
Terms

This glossary is a partial list excerpted from the one on the National Association of REALTORS® (NAR) website and the Real Estate Section of Yahoo Finance. You can go to *www.realtor.com* and click on "Real Estate Glossary" for more. Real estate brokerage is truly dependent on the "lingo"—so have fun.

Acceleration clause A provision in a mortgage that gives the lender the right to demand payment of the entire principal balance if a monthly payment is missed.

Adjustable-rate mortgage (ARM) A mortgage that permits the lender to adjust its interest rate periodically on the basis of changes in a specified index.

Amortization The gradual repayment of a mortgage loan by installments.

Annual percentage rate (APR) The cost of a mortgage stated as a yearly rate; includes such items as interest, mortgage insurance and loan origination fee (points). Use of the APR permits a standard expression of credit costs, which facilitates easy comparison of lenders.

Appraisal A written analysis of the estimated value of a property prepared by a qualified appraiser. As contrasted to a home inspection.

Assumable mortgage A mortgage that can be taken over ("assumed") by the buyer when a home is sold. It is seldom done in today's market place.

Balloon mortgage A mortgage that has level monthly payments that will amortize it over a stated term but that provides for a lump sum payment to be due at the end of an earlier specified term.

Bridge (swing) loan A form of second trust that is collateralized by the borrower's present home (which is usually for sale) in a manner that allows the proceeds to be used for closing on a new house before the present home is sold. Also known as a "swing loan."

Broker A person who, for a commission or a fee, brings parties together and assists in negotiating contracts between them.

Buydown mortgage A temporary buydown is a mortgage on which an initial lump-sum payment is made by any party to reduce a borrower's monthly payments during the first few years of a mortgage. A permanent buydown reduces the interest rate over the entire life of a mortgage.

Cap A provision of an adjustable-rate mortgage (ARM) that limits how much the interest rate or mortgage payments may increase or decrease.

Closing costs Expenses (over and above the price of the property) incurred by buyers and sellers in transferring ownership of a property. Closing costs normally include an origination fee, an attorney's fee, taxes, an amount placed in escrow and charges for obtaining title insurance and a survey. Closing costs percentages will vary according to the area of the country; lenders or Realtors®often provide estimates of closing costs to prospective homebuyers.

Collateral In a home loan, the property is the collateral. The borrower risks losing the property if the loan is not repaid according to the terms of the mortgage or deed of trust.

Commission Payment to a broker for services rendered, such as in the sale or purchase of real property; usually a percentage of the selling price of the property.

Comparables Recent sales of similar properties in nearby areas used to help determine the market value of a property. Also referred to as "comps."

Conforming loan Any loan that meets the qualifications to be purchased by Fannie Mae or Freddie Mac.

Contingency A condition that must be met before a contract is legally binding. For example, home purchasers often include a contingency that specifies that the contract is not binding until the purchaser obtains a satisfactory home inspection report from a qualified home inspector.

Conventional mortgage A mortgage that is not insured or guaranteed by the federal government.

Cost of fund index (COFI) One of the indexes that is used to determine interest rate changes for certain adjustable-rate mortgages. It represents the weighted-average cost of savings, borrowing and advances of financial institutions such as banks and savings and loans.

Credit report A report of an individual's credit history prepared by a credit bureau and used by a lender in determining a loan applicant's creditworthiness.

Deed The legal document conveying title to a property.

Deed of Trust A document that gives a lender the right to foreclose on a piece of property if the borrower defaults on the loan.

Due-on-sale provision A provision in a mortgage that allows the lender to demand repayment in full if the borrower sells the property that serves as security for the mortgage.

Earnest money deposit A deposit made by the potential home buyer to show that they are serious about buying the house.

Easement A right of way giving persons other than the owner access to, or over, a property.

Encroachment An improvement that intrudes illegally on another's property.

Encumbrance Anything that affects or limits the fee simple title to a property, such as mortgages, leases, easements or restrictions.

Equity A homeowner's financial interest in a property. Equity is the difference between the fair market value of the property and the amount still owed on its mortgage and other liens.

Escrow An item of value, money or documents deposited with a third party to be delivered upon the fulfillment of a condition. For example, the deposit by a borrower with the lender of funds to pay taxes and insurance premiums when they become due, or funds or documents may be deposited with an attorney to be disbursed upon the closing of a sale of real estate.

Fannie Mae (Federal National Mortgage Association) Fannie Mae is a New York Stock Exchange company and the largest nonbank financial services company in the world. It operates pursuant to a federal charter and is the nation's largest source of financing for home mortgages. Over the past 30 years, Fannie Mae has provided nearly $2.5 trillion of mortgage financing for over 30 million families.

Federal Housing Administration (FHA) An agency of the U.S. Department of Housing and Urban Development (HUD). Its main activity is the insuring of residential mortgage loans made by private lenders. The FHA sets standards for construction and underwriting but does not lend money or plan or construct housing.

FHA mortgage A mortgage that is insured by the Federal Housing Administration (FHA). Also known as a government mortgage. The loan is made by a private financial institution.

Fixed rate mortgage A mortgage in which the interest rate is fixed for the duration of the loan. You always know what the payments will be. Usually the interest is higher than with an ARM.

Flood insurance Insurance that compensates for physical property damage resulting from flooding. It is required for properties located in federally designated flood areas.

Foreclosure The legal process by which a borrower in default under a mortgage is deprived of their interest in the mortgaged property.

Freddie Mac The Federal Home Loan Mortgage Corporation. This company buys mortgage from lending institutions, pools them with other loans and sells shares to investors.

Good faith estimate An estimate from an institutional lender that shows the costs a borrower will incur, including loan-processing charges and inspection fees.

Gross income The total income of a household before taxes or expenses are subtracted.

Hazard insurance Insurance coverage that compensates for physical damage to a property from fire, wind, vandalism or other hazards. It does not cover personal property, and is almost always required, as a minimum, by the lender.

Home inspection A thorough inspection that evaluates the structural and mechanical condition of a home. This is not the same as an appraisal of property.

Homeowner's Association A nonprofit association that manages the common areas of a planned unit development (PUD) or condominium project. In a condominium project, it has no ownership interest in the common elements. In a PUD project, it holds title to the common elements.

Homeowner's insurance An insurance policy that combines personal liability insurance and hazard insurance coverage for a dwelling and its contents.

HUD 1 statement A document that provides an itemized listing of the funds that are payable at closing. Items that appear on the statement include real estate commissions, loan fees, points and initial escrow amounts. Each item on the statement is represented by a separate number within a standardized numbering system. The totals at the bottom of the HUD 1 statement define the seller's net proceeds and the buyer's net payment at closing. The blank form for the statement is published by the Department of Housing and Urban Development (HUD). The HUD 1 statement is also known as the "closing statement" or "settlement sheet."

Insured conventional loan A loan with less than 20 percent downpayment. The difference is covered by Private Mortgage Insurance (PMI). The PMI can be dropped (with the lender's approval) from your monthly payments when you have established 20 percent equity in your property. You can accomplish this by your payments and the appreciated cash value of your home (as determined by a qualified appraisal).

Interest rate The rate of interest in effect for the monthly payment due.

Lease A written agreement between the property owner and a tenant that stipulates the payment and conditions under which the tenant may possess the real estate for a specified period of time.

Lien A legal claim against a property that must be paid off when the property is sold.

Loan Commitment A promise by a lender or other financial institution to make or insure a loan for a specified amount and on specific terms.

Lock-in A written agreement in which the lender guarantees a specified interest rate if a mortgage goes to closing within a set period of time. The lock-in also usually specifies the number of points to be paid at closing.

Market Value The most probable price a property would bring in an arms-length transaction under normal conditions on the open market.

Maturity The date on which the principal balance of a loan, bond or other financial instrument becomes due and payable.

Mortgage A legal document that pledges a property to the lender as security for payment of a debt.

Mortgage insurance A contract that insures the lender against loss caused by a mortgager's default on a mortgage. Mortgage insurance can be issued by a private company or by a government agency such as the Federal Housing Administration (FHA). Depending on the type of policy, the insurance may cover a percentage of or virtually all of the mortgage loan. See private mortgage insurance (PMI).

Mortgage insurance premium (MIP) The amount paid by a mortgagor for mortgage insurance, either to a government agency such as the Federal Housing Administration (FHA) or to a private mortgage insurance (PMI) company. See private mortgage insurance below.

Mortgagee The lender in a mortgage agreement.

Mortgagor The borrower in a mortgage agreement.

Negative amortization Some adjustable rate mortgages allow the interest rate to fluctuate independently of a required minimum payment. If a borrower makes the minimum payment it may not cover all of the interest that would normally be due at the current interest rate. In essence, the borrower is deferring the interest payment, which is why this is called "deferred interest." The deferred interest is added to the balance of the loan and the loan balance grows larger instead of smaller, which is called negative amortization.

Nonconforming loan A nonconforming loan is any loan that doesn't meet the qualification or is too large to be purchased by Fannie Mae or Freddie Mac.

Note A legal document that requires a borrower to repay a mortgage at a certain interest rate over a specified period of time.

Origination fee A fee paid to a lender for processing a loan application. The origination fee is stated in the form of points. One point is 1 percent of the mortgage amount.

PITI See principal, interest, taxes and insurance (PITI).

Planned unit development (PUD) A project or subdivision that includes common property that is owned and maintained by a homeowner's association for the benefit and use of the individual PUD unit owners.

Point A unit of measurement used for various loan charges; one point equals 1 percent of the amount of the loan.

Preapproval A loosely used term which is generally taken to mean that a borrower has completed a loan application and provided debt, income and savings documentation which an underwriter has reviewed and approved. A preapproval is usually done at a certain loan amount and by making assumptions about what the interest rate will be at the time the loan is actually made, as well as estimates for the amount that will be paid for property taxes and insurance.

Prepayment Any amount paid to reduce the principal balance of a loan before the due date. Payment in full on a mortgage that may result from a sale of the property, the owner's decision to pay off the loan in full or a foreclosure. In each case, prepayment means payment occurs before the loan has been fully amortized.

Prequalification The process of determining how much money a prospective home buyer will be eligible to borrow before they apply for a loan.

Prime rate The interest rate that banks charge to their approved customers. Changes in the prime rate are widely publicized in the news media and are used as the indexes in some adjustable rate mortgages, especially home equity lines of credit.

Principal, interest, taxes and insurance (PITI)T h e four components of a monthly mortgage payment. Principal refers to the part of the monthly payment that reduces the remaining balance of the mortgage. Interest is the fee charged for borrowing money. Taxes and insurance refer to the amounts that are paid into an escrow account each month for property taxes and mortgage and hazard insurance.

Private mortgage insurance (PMI) Mortgage insurance that is provided by a private mortgage insurance company to protect lenders against loss if a borrower defaults. Most lenders generally require PMI for a loan with a loan-to-value (LTV) percentage in excess of 80 percent. This is a recurring monthly charge, reflected in the PITI.

Qualifying ratios Calculations that are used in determining whether a borrower can qualify for a mortgage. They consist of two separate calculations: a housing expense as a percent of income ratio and total debt obligations as a percent of income ratio.

Realtor® A real estate broker or an associate who holds active membership in a local real estate board that is affiliated with the National Association of REALTORS®.

Recording The noting in the registrar's office of the details of a properly executed legal document, such as a deed, a mortgage note, a ratification of a mortgage or an extension of a mortgage, thereby making it part of the public record.

Refinance transaction The process of paying off one loan with the proceeds from a new loan using the same property as security.

Right of first refusal A provision in an agreement that requires the owner of a property to give another party the first opportunity to purchase or lease the property before they offer it for sale or lease to others.

Second mortgage A mortgage that has a lien position subordinate to the first mortgage.

Settlement sheet See HUD 1 statement.

Subordinate loan A second or third mortgage.

Title A legal document evidencing a person's right to or ownership of a property.

Title insurance A policy insuring the owner against loss by reason of defects in the title on a parcel of real estate, other than encumbrance, defects and matters specifically excluded by the policy.

Title search The examination of public records relating to real estate to determine the current state of ownership.

Truth-in-Lending Act A federal law that requires lenders to fully disclose, in writing, the terms and conditions of a mortgage, including the annual percentage rate (APR) and other charges.

Underwriting The process of evaluating a loan application to determine the risk involved for the lender. Underwriting involves an analysis of the borrower's creditworthiness and the quality of the property itself.

VA mortgage A mortgage that is guaranteed by the Department of Veterans Affairs (VA). Also known as a government mortgage. The actual loan however, is made by a private financial institution.

Zoning Regulations that control the use of land within a jurisdiction.

APPENDIX B

Compendium of Useful Internet Sites by Category

Neighborhood and Community Information and Profiles

www.chamberofcommerce.com
This site links to local chamber of commerce chapters all over the country.

www.homefair.com
This site offers information on neighborhoods, schools, moving and more.

www.census.gov
This is the U.S. Census Bureau's website.

Credit Reports

Equifax

www.equifax.com
PO Box 105873
Atlanta, GA 30348
(800) 685-1111

Experian

www.experian.com
PO Box 2104
Allen, TX 75013
(888) 397-3742

Trans Union

www.transunion.com
PO Box 390
Springfield, PA 19064
(800) 916-8800

Central Credit Report Data Bank

www.annualcreditreport.com
Annual Credit Report Request Service
PO Box 105281
Atlanta, GA 30348-5281
(877) 322-8228

Local School Systems

Fairfax County: *www.fcps.k12.va.us*

Loudoun County: *www.loudoun.k12.va.us*

Arlington County: *www.arlington.k12.va.us*

Prince William County: *www.pwcs.edu*

City of Alexandria: *www.acps.k12.va.us*

City of Falls Church: *www.fccps.k12.va.us*

Private Schools

Independent Schools: *www.vais.org*

Private Child Care Centers: *www.daycarevirginia.com*

List of Private Schools: *www.virginiabusiness.com*

Transportation

Washington Metropolitan Area Transit Authority: *www.wmata.com*

Virginia Department of Transportation: *www.vdot.virginia.gov*

MARC TRAIN: *www.mtamaryland.com*

Reston Transportation Information: *www.linkinfo.org*

Virginia Railway Express: *www.vre.org*

Virginia Department of Motor Vehicles:
www.dmv.state.va.us

Shopping

Tyson's Corner Shopping Mall: *www.shoptysons.com*

Potomac Mills Outlets: *www.potomacmills.com*

Crystal City Shopping: *www.crystalcity.com*

Reston Town Center: *www.restontowncenter.com*

Leesburg Outlet Center: *www.outletsonline.com*

Dulles Town Center Mall: *www.shopdullestowncenter.com*

Shopping guide—Washington DC:
www.washington.dc.retailguide.com

Real Estate Sites

Long & Foster, Inc.: *www.longandfoster.com*

My website: *www.callteamworks.com*

APPENDIX C

Handy "To Do" List for Your Move

Moving from one residence to another can be a very time-consuming, stressful and challenging experience, depending on your circumstances. I strongly recommend that you have a plan with a clear timetable detailing your objectives. Obviously the cost, time and effort involved depends on your situation. A 23-year-old bachelor moving from his "bachelor pad" to his new one-bedroom condo may need just a couple of buddies over in the morning to help him load the Ryder truck and unload at the other end. If you are a family of six moving to another city, however, moving is a very big deal and should be approached in a thoughtful, methodical way. The following list contains recommendations from Long and Foster, Inc., for the big move.

8 Weeks Before

❏ If you are relocating because of a job transfer, make sure you know what costs your employer will incur and reimburse.

❏ Dispose of unnecessary items from your attic, basement, storage shed and so on.

❏ Have a detailed floor plan of your next home and determine what furniture will not fit there.

❏ Solicit estimates from moving companies.

❏ Create a file for all of the documents on moving and relevant receipts.

❏ If you're moving out of state or out of your school district, arrange to transfer your children's school records.

❏ Evaluate your possessions. Are there items you should donate to charity? Do you really need all of your stuff? Would you be moving some very low-priority things?

6 Weeks Before

❏ Contact the IRS and/or your CPA for information on what moving expenses are tax deductible.

❏ Notify your friends, relatives, doctors, creditors, subscriptions and the like of your move and your new address.

❏ Locate high-quality healthcare professionals in your new location.

❏ Complete change of address cards from the post office (or via an online service) for banks, charge cards, doctors, dentist, income tax bureaus, Social Security Administration, insurance broker, lawyer, accountant and stockbroker.

❏ Hold a garage sale for low-priority stuff.

❏ Choose a mover and make insurance coverage arrangements.

4 Weeks Before

❏ Assemble in one file all auto licensing and registration documentation; medical, dental and school records; birth certificates; wills, deeds, stock and other financial documentation.

❏ Contact gas, electric, heating oil, water, telephone, cable TV and trash collection companies for service disconnection and connection at your old and new addresses. Also ask for final readings.

❏ Request refunds on unused homeowner's insurance, security deposits and prepaid cable service.

❏ Contact insurance companies to arrange for coverage in your new home.

2 Weeks Before

❏ Arrange special transport for your pets.

❏ Service your car for the trip.

❏ Contact your moving company and review arrangements for your move.

APPENDIX D

Phone Lists

Telephone

Verizon (toll-free): (800) 483-4000

Verizon: (540) 954-6222

Utilities

Dominion VA Power: (888) 667-3000

Northern VA Electric: (888) 335-0500

Northern Neck Electric: (800) 243-2860

City of Manassas: (703) 257-8219

PEPCO-DC: (800) 424-8028

Washington Gas: (703) 750-1000

Columbia Gas: (800) 543-8911

Water

Alexandria: (703) 549-7080

Arlington: (703) 228-3636

Culpepper: (540) 727-3423

Fairfax: (703) 698-5800

Fauquier: (540) 349-2092

Warrenton: (540) 347-1101

Falls Church: (703) 248-5071

Prince William: (703) 335-7900

Spotsylvania: (540) 898-2053

Herndon: (703) 435-6814

Leesburg: (703) 771-2701

Loudoun: (703) 771-1095

Manassas: (703) 257-8219

Appendix E

Preferred Partners

ONE OF THE SECRETS TO SUCCESSFUL REAL ESTATE SALES...

The Most Trusted Name in Real Estate Settlements

DILIGENCE, EXPERIENCE, CONVENIENCE, INTEGRITY.

Alexandria
(703) 519-7600
(703) 519-9471 FAX
Annandale
(703) 642-6100
(703) 642-6142 FAX
Arlington
(703) 351-0300
(703) 351-9978 FAX
Ashburn
703-726-9222
(703) 726-9368 FAX
Burke
(703) 239-9600
(703) 239-0605 FAX
Centreville
(703) 818-8600
(703) 803-2867 FAX
Culpeper
(540) 829-9000
(540) 829-7825 FAX
Fredericksburg
(540) 372-4100
(540) 372-4114 FAX
Lake Ridge
(703) 491-9600
(703) 492-7494 FAX
Lorton
(703) 495-9600
(703) 493-9302 FAX

Manassas
(703) 396-8838
(703) 396-8809 FAX
McLean
(703) 903-9600
(703) 903-9606 FAX
Oakton
(703) 242-9600
(703) 242-0725 FAX
Potomac Falls
(703) 421-3300
(703) 421-6353 FAX
Reston
(703) 742-9600
(703) 742-9698 FAX
Reston-Wiehle
(703) 437-1777
(703) 437-4344 FAX
Springfield
(703) 451-6600
(703) 451-1181 FAX
Stafford
703-288-1747
703-288-1797 FAX
Winchester
540-723-0662
540-723-0664 FAX
Bethesda
(301) 654-9800
(301) 654-8598 FAX

Rockville
(301) 230-0070
(301) 230-2536 FAX
Gaithersburg
(240) 683-4850
(240) 683-6676 FAX
Silver Spring
(301) 680-0200
(301) 680-2043 FAX
Washington, D.C.
(202) 966-0550
(202) 966-5250 FAX
Bilingual Department
(703) 642-6100
Realtors Hotline
(703) 660-5150

RGS
COMMERCIAL

Fairfax, Virginia
(703) 383-5833
(703) 383-3919 FAX
Bethesda, Maryland
(240) 395-0470
(240) 395-0471 FAX
Clinton, Maryland
(301) 877-1100
(301) 877-8141 FAX

Appendix E

INNOVATIVE SOLUTIONS
FROM A LEADING
MORTGAGE LENDER

Prosperity
Mortgage
Company

CARL GAMLEN
HOME MORTGAGE CONSULTANT
Phone: 703-963-6036 Pager: 703-612-4936
Alt Phone: 703-433-7418
Carl.gamlem@wellsfargo.com

WE OFFER:

* THE WELLS FARGO SMART FIT HOME MORTGAGE PRODUCT LINE
WITH A FIXED TERM INTEREST-ONLY LINE OF CREDIT FROM
$100,000 TO $3 MILLION

* RELATIONSHIP ARMs/LIBOR ARMs

*JUMBO AND CONVENTIONAL LOANS-FLEXIBLE DOWN PAYMENT
OPTION- INTEREST ONLY FEATURES ON MANY PROGRAMS

*NEW CONSTRUCTION PROGRAMS

*EXTENDED NIGHT AND WEEKEND HOURS TO HELP YOU TAKE
ADVANTAGE OF OUR FLEXIBLE FINANCING

Talk with your Wells Fargo Home Mortgage Consultant Today